A LIFE EMPOWERED

A LIFE EMPOWERED

A Guide to Self-Mastery, Freedom and Inner Peace

JEAN-PIERRE CLAUDE

FURTHER SHORE
PUBLISHING

*For anyone who has ever felt that something was missing,
even when everything seemed to be in place.*

*And for you, J.
For walking every step of this journey beside me,
and for giving me the freedom and courage
to explore, grow and simply be.*

*"Let go of the past, let go of the future, let go of the
present, and cross over to the further*

shore of existence."
— The Buddha

"The Kingdom of God is within you."
— Jesus

CONTENTS

PART ONE

A Simple Path to Wholeness

CHAPTER ONE

The Cup

THERE ONCE WAS A YOUNG man whose parents gave him a cup, and they told him, like their parents taught them, and like their grandparents taught their parents, that as long as he kept his cup full, eternal happiness would be his.

Each day he went down to the stream, as everyone else did, to fill his cup. But after a little while, every cup would again be empty, to everyone's dismay. Day after day the people of the village would return to the stream and the well, each time hoping that their cups would remain full this time, but the cups never did.

There were myths of special fountains that would keep his cup full, but the young man never managed to find these, despite great efforts. There were also many stories of special rituals that would keep his cup full, but these did not seem to work either. No matter what he tried, he would approach his cup after a little while with great anticipation, only to find it empty again.

Eventually the young man gave up on this pursuit and decided to leave his town, with his cup in his satchel. He walked far and wide, learning all he could about the world.

Eventually he came across an old man who seemed to be filled with a joy for life. The young man thought that the man must have found a way to keep his cup filled and immediately asked him about it.

Instead of answering, the old man asked to see the young man's cup. He held it up to the light and pointed to the bottom of the stem: it was open.

At first, the young man panicked, thinking his cup had been damaged during his journey. But the old man smiled and pulled his own vessel from his saddlebag. It was formed in exactly the same way.

"Funnels are not meant to be filled the way cups are," the old man explained. "You will always feel empty if you try to fill the unfillable." Realising the truth, the young man finally found the peace he had always been seeking.

With his newfound knowledge, he returned to his town, and was surprised at how everyone in town was missing this obvious truth which had become such a plain fact to him. He saw people running around in ignorance, trying to fill the unfillable.

From that day on he decided to share his insight with anyone who would stop and ask him why he was not trying to fill his cup anymore, yet he himself overflowed with streams of joy and peace.

When the villagers would gather around him at sunset to listen, when the cookfires were just starting to warm the twilight air, he would wait for total silence, then slowly lean into the light, and at last begin his telling.

"There once was a young man whose parents gave him a cup…"

CHAPTER TWO

My Story

THE QUESTION THAT HAUNTED ME for years was simple: Why, despite having everything, did I feel so empty?

It's not like I had hit some sort of rock bottom. This isn't one of *those* stories, exactly.

I've had a pretty normal life. Good, even.

I did well at school.

I was in a "model", traditional family who all attended church together on Sundays.

I got the finance degree like my sister, and secured a respectable corporate job at a large accountancy firm.

My friends and family approved; they saw the comfortable life, the checked boxes, and the undeniable success.

I remember staring out the train window on the ride home from a long day at the office, watching the lights streak past, and being gripped by the crushing realisation that despite being ticked, the boxes were nevertheless hollow.

I'd *followed* the formula, I'd done *everything* they'd asked of me... and yet here I was, knowing in my heart that something was wrong.

I knew I had everything to be grateful for, and still I did not feel whole. If you'd asked me what was missing, I would not have been able to tell you.

And beyond that, I could not reconcile what I'd heard in church all those years with my inner guidance. The way I had been told the world and the hereafter worked simply did not add up, which left me with even more questions.

At first, I thought it was just me or my community, but as I continued my search, I soon realised I wasn't alone in this feeling. There was a general unease or unhappiness in the background of society at large, and it was consistent in different countries, different cities, different cultures, different religions, different socioeconomic groups.

There seemed to be a universal seeking within everyone, like a seed that had been planted and was desperately in need of something in order for it to grow.

This led me to broaden my horizons, trying to understand different perspectives on life, interacting with people with different views from the norm. I was so eager to uncover the answers that I wished for more hours in the day just to go through all the books, courses and other writings. I sifted and sorted through everything I encountered, but also through my own thoughts, insights and conclusions, and whenever I found something that resonated with me, I kept it.

I was collecting pieces of a puzzle, with no image on the box to guide me, no idea what it might be building towards. I kept searching and fitting and building, until one day it started forming a picture, one that grew clearer and clearer as I continued my search.

At first it was a broader understanding of how everything fits together—our lives here on Earth, our true purpose, and who we truly are. Then, on one autumn morning, as I watched the rain patter against my window, it all clicked at once, as if the clouds had parted and a solitary beam of sunlight had broken through.

Having watched the dramatic change playing out in my life since that morning, I decided that this knowledge of how to bridge the gap between the life we live and the life we yearn for felt like something I had to share with the world. By bringing together the pieces of the puzzle into this book, my sincerest wish is that it will ignite or further your own internal knowing so you can claim your life of peace, joy and love.

CHAPTER THREE

Engaging with This Book

I WROTE THESE NOTES PRIMARILY for myself as I embarked on a journey to embody love, joy and peace. While I don't hold any of these ideas as absolute truth, I can tell you that it was a shift in my perspective, the one outlined in these pages, that helped me find what I was looking for. As I grow, so do my insights, but the core remains steadfast because it's anchored in something beyond the temporary—something eternal and unchanging.

Love.

That being said, the specifics of the journey will look different to each of us, as we all have different starting points, backgrounds, things to learn and unlearn. Therefore, I invite you to explore with me the core of what lies in these pages. To do so, I ask you to read not only with your eyes, but also with your heart, and to write the words in this book *with* me. Make them your own. Take notes. Take pauses. Reflect on them and decide what is valuable to you. Use your own Light and guidance to illuminate your path and come to your own insights.

Throughout the book you will find *Your Practice* sections that distil the key insights into reflections you can carry with you. These invite you to pause and check in with yourself. There is also a space at the back of the book for your own notes, and I would encourage you to use it. The insights that matter most will often be the ones that arise from within as you read.

The book is structured to principally explore how we can embody peace, joy and love—both in general and in specific areas of our lives, such as relationships, careers and physical well-being. You are welcome to jump to or revisit any of these sections, depending on what is most relevant to your experience right now. However, my recommendation is to work chronologically through the book from start to finish. If you wish to visit a later section first, please first read "Core Concepts" in the "Knowing Ourselves" section, which gives an overview of the terminology that we'll be using throughout the book.

My wish for you is that you embody that which you seek, and if our journey through these pages serves that intention, then I am honoured to share a part of your own unique, beautiful story with you.

Thank you for joining me on this journey.

Are you ready to take the first step with me?

PART TWO

Knowing Ourselves

CHAPTER FOUR

The Search for Meaning

IN MY OPENING STORY I told you about the universal search for something more that is planted within humans.

When I say *universal*, I am not only talking about people from all races, cultures and traditions, but also about people from different times in the history of humankind.

Every human is born with a connection to the non-physical. In fact, you are *a part* of the non-physical because you are the materialisation of it; an extension of it.

You might not believe this yourself, and that is okay. We will explore why I say this and what it means a little later on.

For now, grant me that it's true: every person has some sort of connection to something non-physical. Some call it a soul, or a spirit, but we are all connected to it, and whether you are aware of it or not, in every moment of your life you are situated in a relative position to that non-physical part of you. Some people find themselves, on average, in close proximity to that part of them, while for others it's very remote, almost impossible to believe, mainly because it *seems* impossible to experience. It is the gravitational pull of this intangible connection that drives humans to search for meaning in their everyday experiences.

We have seen this search echoed throughout history, particularly in the lives of major spiritual and religious figures. For example, although born a prince, the Buddha realised that conditioned experiences could not provide lasting joy or alleviation from emotional suffering. Even though society often views wealth, luxury and riches as the things that bring fulfilment, these societal beliefs simply do not lead to true, pure joy. Some may profess that it is not their belief, yet their actions and view of themselves and others tell a different story.

We see a similar story to the Buddha's in Francis of Assisi. He was a wealthy young man and he was said to have spent money lavishly in his early years, but then he started to change and lose interest in the world outside. He withdrew more and more from society as his focus shifted to obtaining spiritual enlightenment. Like the Buddha before him, he also grew disillusioned with the world he saw around him. Both of these men sought something more even though they ostensibly already had everything you might need to live a happy life—by the standards of society, at least.

Perhaps one of the most-recognised historical and religious figures, Jesus Christ, understood and often touched upon people's search for something more, something that would give them the fulfilment they seek. He likened that feeling of yearning for more to *thirst* when he said: "If anyone is thirsty, let him come to me and drink!" This was to say that he would share his knowledge about what brings true fulfilment with those who were searching for it.

This search continues to be seen across the world today by the sheer number of people who follow religion and spirituality as part of that pursuit of wholeness. Even in the scientific communities we can see the need to understand the role of humans in the universe, which is also why people are fascinated by the idea of life on this planet and its origins, and the question of whether life could be found on other planets. This is part of wanting to understand who we are and what role we play in the greater scheme of things.

Isaac Newton, one of the best-known scientists in history, was famously in search of that greater part of existence when he said: "So then gravity may put the planets into motion, but without the Divine Power it could never put them into such a circulating motion, as they have about the sun." This great figure is remembered best for his scientific contributions, but it's often forgotten that a not insignificant portion of his work was dedicated to the search for the alchemical philosophers' stone, something that symbolises life, rejuvenation and enlightenment.

Similarly, biologists are fascinated by the human body and its mechanisms as they seek to understand it better and thereby further medicine and preserve life. This intense focus exists because the body is at the base of the identity of most humans. As a psychiatrist, Carl Jung also wanted to define the human identity, and much of his work focused on what he described as the urge towards self-realisation.

As we can see, the human mind, in one form or another, is always in search of what will make it feel whole. Central to that search for fulfilment is understanding *who you are*.

If you have spent your life searching, striving and pushing for external fulfilment, know that every step has been valuable. Each one has brought you closer to this point, closer to your spiritual home.

Now we turn the search inward, where the answer has always resided.

Are you ready to take this journey with me?

CHAPTER FIVE

Core Concepts

THERE ARE A NUMBER OF CONCEPTS that I will use throughout this book. Some of these will already have meaning to you, so it is important to clarify how they will be used for the purpose of our discussion.

Consciousness

When I speak of Consciousness, I am not referring to a state of awareness of your human brain. In this human form, consciousness is a function of your mind, but in terms of the capitalised Consciousness, we are talking about the existence of sentient awareness that is beyond your own mind. This transcendent awareness is the origin of all, and all is part of Consciousness, the "All-That-Is".

In the Bible, when Moses asks the burning bush about its identity, the answer he receives is "I am who I am" — this is raw Consciousness, almost frustratingly self-referential, without defined form or individual identity as we understand that concept from the perspective of the human mind. In modern spirituality, this is often referred to as "Source Energy" or simply "Source".

The Self

As a subcategory of Consciousness, there is also the concept of the Self.

Psychiatrist Carl Jung referred to the Self as "the archetype of transcendent wholeness," but for our purposes here, we shall think of it as the specifically focused extensions of Consciousness, which itself is that non-materialised part of you. That is, the specific focused stream of Consciousness which gave rise to you in this human form is your "Self". I often also refer to it as your True Self. However, do not think of this as a static object or a ghost in the machine. Think of it as your eternal frequency—a continuous, flowing stream of consciousness that retains its unique resonance even as it evolves.

Now, when we speak of the *identity* of an extension of Consciousness, this does not quite fit the human mind's idea of identity. Consciousness is indescribable using concrete human ideas and definitions, but please bear with me here.

Let's say that assigning a specific identity to one focused stream of Consciousness is like identifying a specific portion of the ocean and giving it a name, like the Atlantic Ocean. It is still part of the ocean in every way, and the ocean is part of it; you have just defined it in certain terms, given it a certain name, an identity. But we all realise that there isn't really a concrete object that is the Atlantic Ocean. It's more like a "division of convenience" that allows us to talk about a specific area. That is sort of how it is with identifying the Self.

This is what many have intuitively pointed to when they speak of the soul, or what others refer to as the "Higher Self".

The Avatar

The next term that you'll see me use often is *the avatar*. This refers to a focused part of the Self that has become manifest in this world. I also refer to it at times as the human form, the form, or the self (not capitalised). This encompasses all the parts that make up your physical experience as a human being, such as the body, the senses, the mind, and so on. It is the temporary, focused part of the Self in the material form.

The Self is the named portion of the ocean, but the avatar is just a single wave—a temporary form that is distracted by the wind and is terrified of crashing, all while forgetting that its entire essence is the limitless water of Consciousness.

The Integrated Self

Our ultimate goal is not just to understand the Self and the self, but to learn how to align them. This alignment is what I call the Integrated Self. This occurs when the avatar uses its mind to focus in a way that is in agreement with the focused perspective of the Self. In other words, the thoughts, focus and perspective of the avatar and the Self overlap, resonate and harmonise for *that moment*.

Carl Jung's description of the integrated self was "indistinguishable from a divine image," which is pretty accurate even for our purposes (even though he was speaking from a psychological perspective, and we are speaking more from a metaphysical perspective). Jung also described self-realisation as "the incarnation of God" —keep this in mind for later.

I will often use *aligned* (and the related term *alignment*) as shorthand for the Integrated Self. This describes the moment when you are aligning the focus, perspective and emotional states of the avatar, the Self, and by extension, Consciousness.

Inner Peace

When you are living as the Integrated Self, the emotional state which you enter in that moment we will refer to as your Inner Peace. This is a place of pure joy, peace, wholeness, love and so forth. This is the emotional state that all humans seek to achieve, whether they realise it or not. This is the object of their wanting, the reason for their lifelong search. This reminds me of what Jesus called the "Kingdom of God" or the "Kingdom of Heaven" and what the Buddha called "Nirvana", the place of enlightenment. This place the Buddha described as "unborn, unrivalled, secure from attachment, undecaying and unstained. This condition is indeed reached by me which is deep, difficult to see, difficult to understand, tranquil, excellent, beyond the reach of mere logic, subtle, and to be realised only by the wise."

I also refer to this state as your *natural* state or *true* state, as it is the state which naturally arises when the mind of the avatar is not obstructing it.

This is the place we will seek together.

CHAPTER SIX

The Integrated Self: Reclaiming Your Identity

NOW THAT WE HAVE ESTABLISHED the concepts of Consciousness, the Self and the avatar, we can begin to answer the fundamental question: **Who am I?**

Deconstructing the Avatar's False Identity

In trying to answer that question, many people will describe their roles: they are a brother, a son, a mother, or a father; they have a specific occupation, such as a doctor or a lawyer; they are a golfer, a runner, or a cancer survivor. In other words, they describe their identity through their relationships with others, through how they earn an income, through their past experiences, the condition of their body or how they spend their time.

But there is something more fundamental to our identities, something underlying those roles. You remain who you are in essence even though the descriptor that you use changes. You are still you, even if in this moment you are acting as an employee as you wrap up the last of your job tasks for the day, and later you step into the role as a parent when you walk through your front door after work to help your kids with their homework, and even later you assume the role of spouse when you go out for date night. You are still you even when you retire, or when your kids leave the house, or when you are widowed, aren't you? That tells us that these descriptors of our jobs and relationship roles, while useful as everyday categories, do not truly strike at the heart of our identities. They are not complete. They describe what you do, not who you are.

So if you are not defined by the roles that you play every day, who are you then underneath all of that?

Some answer that you are your experiences. It is often said that you are the sum of your experiences, by which we mean those things you live through and take in via your senses, accumulated across your lifetime. Even though your senses definitely add to your experience here, we can safely say that they don't define who you truly are. The feeling of being "you" persists beyond sensory input. Even without much sensory input, you don't cease to be. In fact, I've had the fascinating experience of floating in a sensory deprivation tank at a local spa, and while the feeling coming over you after a while is rewarding, I can confirm that the total experience was not life-altering in any meaningful way. I was still "me" even with no external stimuli. You are not any more or any less dependent on external stimuli to be who you are.

Okay, so what else could impart identity to us?

Emotions are more internal than the senses, so perhaps we can look there. Alas, although emotions are very real and certainly have a big impact on your experience of life, what you feel does not define who you are, as these can change from moment to moment. Once more, you continue to be you whether you are joyful or angry; you still exist even though the various emotions feel completely different.

If you are not your emotions, then perhaps you are your thoughts. That certainly seems very ingrained, like it is getting to the core of who you are. After all, it is only through your thoughts that you are even able to contemplate your identity in the first place! René Descartes famously declared "I think, therefore I am" as the first, most basic principle of his philosophy. Most certainly your thoughts are central to your experience here, because it is through thoughts that you make your decisions, that you have opinions on the information that your senses provide to you, that you can even hope to understand any part of the world around you. And yet, you can sit in stillness and be without thought, and still you do not cease to be. At night, when you enter your sleep or dream state and your thoughts quiet, you still are who you are. Even in dreams, when you may step into a completely different life, one which only makes sense at the time and quickly evaporates in the light of morning, you continue to be you. The thoughts about yourself, however, are the foundation of your avatar, or who you think you are.

The Anchor of Awareness

So what remains between all of these different components or states of our experience?

When your relationship or role in society changes, what remains the same? If your sensory perceptions change or go away, what is it that sticks around? When your emotions are rising and falling and changing from moment to moment, what is it that anchors you? When you are thinking a variety of thoughts, what remains constant irrespective of the kind of thought that you are having, or even whether you are having a thought or not? If you are merely looking at an object and you have no thoughts about it, what still remains? How do you even know whether you are thinking a thought or not?

You see, underlying all of these things is an awareness. You can think of it as the observer behind the things that you perceive, be it a thought, a dream, an emotion or a sensation. That awareness is omnipresent, even if your mind does not focus on it. In other words, it does not need to be acknowledged to exist or to be present. It simply is. In the Hebrew Bible, the personal name of God revealed to Moses is "I am that I am" which does not have a description apart from mere being. This is pure Consciousness.

It is that same Consciousness that focuses in various ways, into various forms, through a very specific focus that forms the basis of life, both yours and mine. What's more, it is the same life-giving force that gives life to the plants and the animals, and although the intentions behind this focus differ for flora and fauna compared to people, the essence of the Consciousness at the very core remains the same. It is from this understanding that the concept of the Oneness arises that you may have heard about (referred to as *henosis* by ancient Greek philosophers). In other words, there is a singular Consciousness that focuses in various ways, but the Consciousness itself remains one concept when you look at the bigger picture, one "entity", you might say, and that is why everything is often described as being interconnected.

Reconciling the Avatar and the Self

At this point you may be wondering how this is relevant to your day-to-day life, where you are dealing with very real and tangible things, and where you feel like you are facing it all as a single, disconnected human. Whether it is ultimately mere perception or not, it *feels real*. The point in giving this introduction, which is a very high-level discussion, is to remind you (because you will know this in your being) that you are more than just your body. That is fundamental to many of the concepts that we shall explore together within these pages.

Let me clarify from the beginning that I am not discounting the value of the avatar (also sometimes called the ego or persona) as part of the life experience. It obviously has an important role to play for the purposes of Consciousness. But since all people in this human form already know what it is to identify with the avatar, and most people overly or solely identify with it, and do not incorporate all of their True Selves into their life experience, the emphasis of this book is to help you understand more of the lesser-known part of yourself, to bring into your life more of that part of your being in order to unify Consciousness with the avatar.

This is how you reach the wholeness you're looking for.

Building Your Relationship with Inner Peace

The path to unification starts with the commitment to your True Self. This relationship is the single most important choice you will ever make. You need to reconcile your mind with that inner knowing that there is more to life than what you can perceive through just the avatar. Many people have already taken that first step. Through their practice of religion or spirituality, they accept that there is something beyond what they experience with their physical senses. For the purposes of our exploration in this book, this acknowledgement of a reality beyond the physical senses is a particularly valuable contribution.

This integrated approach focuses on aligning the avatar and the Self to empower you and lead you to Inner Peace, a perspective that stands in contrast to one that may see you as separate and subservient to a higher power. This journey is one of unlearning and rediscovery. It's less about adopting new beliefs and more about releasing old ones that no longer serve you. This process rarely happens overnight and it's a journey of self-mastery that will look different for everyone. Each limiting belief you shed, regardless of its depth, is a fundamental step towards rediscovering what you're truly reaching for.

Your new foundation is the realisation that you are the result, the manifestation, of the focusing of Consciousness, and even though you are focused Consciousness, you are still part of the greater Consciousness.

The Value of Focused Consciousness

You are not worth more or less than Consciousness or than any other focused points of Consciousness; you are a part of it, after all, and so is everyone (and everything) else. Consciousness, however focused, simply is. Nothing more, nothing less. You can find great comfort in the knowledge that you are not alone in this, and the attention of Consciousness still remains on you and flows through you. It *is* you. It will remain even one day when you are no longer expressing through this avatar. When your time as this avatar has ended (what we traditionally call death), you will remain part of Consciousness, but a newly expanded Consciousness.

Why expanded? Because of the time spent focused into the avatar you think of as yourself, where new perspectives and experiences were gathered up lovingly to be added to the greater whole.

In essence, once you truly know these things, you can start to build a relationship with the part of Consciousness that is focused into this body as you—i.e. the Self. When you meet up with Self, you enter that aligned state, or that place of Inner Peace—what the Buddha frequently referred to as the "hidden treasure within." It is that wholeness that every person seeks, not because you require redemption, but because of the joy, peace and love that rediscovery brings.

Your experience is completely different when you care about being aligned to Self and are using that as a foundation from which to launch your life experience going forward. This is the only stable foundation on which to build your life.

How Do You Build a Relationship with Inner Peace?

How do you start to build a relationship with a person or a concept after acknowledging their existence? Just like when you meet someone new, you get to know them by spending time with them. Because the Self exists beyond the physical realm, it is not through the physical senses that you generally come to know your Self. You need to meet your Self where you can connect with it, which is in your state of Inner Peace.

In this resistance-free and tranquil state you align in perspective with Self, and establish emotional resonance with Consciousness. This is not a new concept. In the Bible, for example, certain emotional states are equated to being in harmony with Consciousness (to put it in my own words)—emotional states like love, joy, peace and so on.

Your emotional state tells you where you are relative to your Inner Peace. This reminds me of the teaching of Buddha which says, "But if he has removed all greed and his mind is pure and peaceful, he is very close to me though he be thousands of miles away." It is about returning to your natural state, which is also the natural state of Self.

Being centred in your Inner Peace is the point where an alignment occurs between your mind and the focused Consciousness (Self), and given that the Self is still part of Consciousness, this means that you then sync up with pure Consciousness. Depending on how much you allow yourself to sync up in this way, you can tune into the perspective, understanding and energy of Consciousness. This is the perspective of the Integrated Self.

It is through becoming sufficiently aware of your relativity to your Inner Peace that you can begin to know it, and integrate it into your daily life. Once you have deliberately tasted the sweetness of alignment, nothing else will do; you will realise that there truly is no replacement for the emotional state of your Inner Peace. The teachings of the Buddha describe it as "a land of peace, a refuge for those who suffer and who are in sorrow and agony."

PART THREE

Self-Mastery in Practice

CHAPTER SEVEN

The Journey Inward

WHEN STARTING THE INWARD JOURNEY, know that you already have everything required, in this moment, to enter your place of Inner Peace.

A common misconception is that self-realisation must be found, earned, or collected outside of you. But self-realisation is not a distant destination; it's a state accessible to you now, throughout your life's journey.

Self-realisation is simply another way to think of the knowledge and ability to enter your Inner Peace, which is to say that you are able to let go of the resistance and "suffering" introduced by the mind. It is a return of the container (your avatar) to the Light (your Self, your essence). This echoes what the Buddha spoke of as "hidden behind the discriminating mind, they possessed a pure mind of Enlightenment which is their true nature."

Even those unaware of their true nature or the practice of directing the mind may occasionally enter their Inner Peace, but this is more a chance occurrence than a deliberate alignment. But if their average proximity to their Inner Peace is distant, they may enter it very seldom, if ever, remaining in a position of strong identification with the avatar alone for long periods of time.

Of course, even if you stumble upon it now and then, if you do not know to look for it, it is also difficult to *stay* close to, or in your Inner Peace for very long. Without understanding *how* you enter it, how do you expect to maintain that thought-resonance with your Inner Peace?

Therefore, a helpful way to think of self-realisation is to:

- be aware of your proximity to your Inner Peace,
- understand that you reach and maintain alignment through directing the mind and shifting your perspective, and
- apply your will to be in alignment as often and for as long as possible.

As you then practise being in alignment more often and for longer periods at a time, your average emotional state starts to shift over time and you grow *generally* closer to your Inner Peace.

Another common misconception is expecting those who pursue self-realisation to never experience thoughts that lead to anger, annoyance or frustration. In other words, expecting their minds to only generate thoughts that resonate with their Inner Peace.

From our discussion above, it should be clear, however, that people who are further along in their self-realisation are still people. They've simply mastered the art of non-identification with passing thoughts and have practised directing their focus with intention to maintain their "balance". It truly is the mastery of a skill, which is why it is available to everyone.

Valuing your self-mastery leads you to seek a swift return to your natural state, as you want to step back into your power and live a directed life. You don't want to deny what is, but you want to build the skill to face what crosses your path from that stable platform of your Inner Peace.

Also, as you become more accustomed to the feeling of being in your Inner Peace, the contrast when you are outside of it starts feeling more pronounced. Think of how much more bitter a sip of coffee can be if you've just had the sweetest of sweets a few moments before.

Those who pursue self-mastery understand that their emotional state reflects their proximity to their Inner Peace, leading them to pay closer attention to their feelings. This heightened awareness can make feelings of discord or resistance feel more intense. However, that should not be seen as a flaw or something to overcome, but rather as the result of a shift in your emotional weather, helping you to course-correct as you go. It is through this awareness that you can start to cultivate a life rooted in joy, regardless of what crosses your path.

Why is Alignment the Path to Joy?

The single most valuable thing that anyone ever seeks is feeling at peace and joyful within themselves.

Many people look for external things to change their state from unhappiness to joy, but you can't make lasting changes to your emotional state this way.

As a matter of fact, nothing external will make you happy for very long.

When you are in a place of wanting, you may think that you would be happy just as soon as you get that new car, or own your own house, or get that promotion, or meet "the one", or finish writing that novel that's been at the back of your mind for a decade. These things are sometimes seen as the building blocks of your own personal Yellow Brick Road that will get you to *happily ever after*.

But that is a mirage, a false promise.

The truth is that these things, these markers of success, can change your short-term emotional state (your emotional weather) in a sort of honeymoon period, but long-term, lasting and deeply fulfilling joy does not come from external factors like these, but from an integration with Self. It is only by aligning the head and the heart that you can uncover a deeper joy, and your experience will change in response to the internal changes.

Why is Lasting Joy an Inside Job?

When referring to joy here, I mean something deeper than experiencing happiness for a short while, which is how the short-term happiness works that we derive from something external. The positive "spike" in the emotional state we get from external achievement does not last very long. Then we start thinking of the next thing that may give us another "fix" of happiness.

But the joy I am referring to here is an emotional state that remains irrespective of external factors. In other words, no matter what is happening in your life, you can enter this place of peace, love and wholeness.

Now, people will often argue with this notion, saying that they cannot possibly enter such a state of Inner Peace given everything that's happening or going wrong in their lives at that moment, which is of course a counter-productive stance to take if you want to direct your life and bring forth better experiences in your future moments. Thinking like that is really just a way to argue for your own limitations.

Remember that the skill to direct your thoughts is something that you haven't necessarily deliberately practised before, and you have to have patience with yourself in learning this new skill, but you can do it. You can learn to think in ways which take you back to your heart's natural state—that state of the Self: Inner Peace.

Taking Steps from Wholeness

In many places I will remind you how your life is a journey that is made up of many moments, and this is one of those places. You can only walk in the direction that you want to go in if your steps take you in that direction. And it is only when you are empowered in the moment that you can take a step that is pointing towards what you *truly* want, as you have the vision and insight into what you *really* want and you have access to your inner guidance.

It is as simple as the distinction between:

- taking steps from a place of peace and wholeness, where you move on to more experiences for your expansion and growth, and

- taking steps from a place of wanting to compensate for what you feel is lacking, which cannot lead to fulfilment.

You simply cannot take enough action to compensate for the emptiness left by spending life outside of your Inner Peace.

Many try to do just that, either to address the uncomfortable background feeling of being unfulfilled, or to address more acute negative feelings such as insecurity, unworthiness, anger, and so on. People often try to numb that *general* feeling of unease by finding ways to distract themselves from it through things such as drugs and medications, food, television, creating drama, sex, and so on. These things then act as distractions from that ongoing feeling of general unease, which might seem to work in the short term, but does nothing to address the root cause of the problem.

When it comes to more acute or intense unwanted feelings, you may look to more directed action in an attempt to soothe that discord within. In this case you may, for example, try to compensate for a feeling of insecurity by becoming a people-pleaser, which you *think* will leave you feeling more worthy because you feel valued by someone else. However, now that feeling of wholeness is dependent on someone else's opinion of you.

Although the one form of emotional unease is more subtle than the other, both dissolve upon entering the aligned state.

It's worth pointing out here that there is never a point where expansion stops. That is also why it is part of your essence to grow, to see more, to know more, to experience more, and to create. It's part of Consciousness and it's part of

You. In other words, being here in this material (physical) container of the human body is expansion.

Becoming self-realised does not have to mean that you stand still and become obsessed with the metaphysical, or just sit and contemplate it all day, although this may be what some people want for their experience. People seem to have this picture in their minds of a self-realised person as a monk who just sits and meditates all day. While that *could* be a way that someone achieves and expresses their self-realisation, it is by no means the only way that it plays out in real life.

Yes, you can be a mother of two who also has a career, but who embodies self-realisation, because she knows who she truly is, and has an intimate relationship with her Inner Peace. She remains in close proximity to it, and looks at life predominantly from the perspective of the Integrated Self.

In other words, just because you are still active in the physical world does not mean that you have to be ruled by the physical, just like living in a self-realised way does not mean you must lose yourself in the deep waters of the metaphysical. Your first priority can and should be seeking alignment with Self, and then you go out into the world and play the physical game that you came to play.

You came here to have a *physical experience*, and to engage on the physical level, but you always are and always will be part of much more than just your physical body. When you integrate the physical self with your Consciousness Self, you step into the power that you knew would be there to support you on your physical journey.

When you try to soldier on without that power, you will always feel that something integral to you is missing — like a background uneasiness that you will have a very hard time explaining. The truth is that most people struggle with this feeling, and it will never go away until they integrate with the Self. You will always be aware of your proximity to your Inner Peace, whether you have the vocabulary to explain it or not.

That is not a bug, it's a feature.

YOUR PRACTICE
Insights for Application

This chapter looks at your identity as focused Consciousness expressing through the avatar, and shows how building a relationship with your Self is the foundation of embodying wholeness.

Self-Realisation is Available Now

Self-realisation is not a distant, earned destination; it's the simple knowledge and ability to enter your Inner Peace by letting go of resistance introduced by the mind.

Acknowledge the Container and the Light

Think of the journey as a return of the container (your avatar) to the Light (your Self). This means embracing your physical form while grounding your identity in your eternal essence.

Define Your Mastery

Self-mastery comes down to three things:

1. Awareness of your proximity to your Inner Peace.
2. Understanding that alignment is reached by directing the mind and shifting your perspective.

3. Applying your intention to remain in alignment as often and for as long as possible.

Shift Your Emotional Climate

Consistently practising alignment shifts your average emotional state over time, drawing you generally closer to your Inner Peace. This is why non-aligned states feel more pronounced as you progress.

Lasting Change is an Inside Job

Nothing external (money, careers, relationships) can provide lasting, deeply fulfilling joy. The deeper joy you're looking for is found by turning inward.

Steps from Wholeness

Notice whether your actions are coming from an empowered state (wholeness/peace) or a compensatory one (lacking/emptiness). You cannot take enough action to compensate for emptiness.

CHAPTER EIGHT

Bridging the Gap to Wholeness

The Practical Application of Consciousness

YOU MAY BE WONDERING HOW you can put the power of Consciousness to use in your day-to-day life. It's one thing to understand that you're more than your body, but it's another to embody that knowledge and apply it in the physical world.

Applying the techniques as described in this *Self-Mastery in Practice* section of the book, you can begin to incorporate Consciousness in your daily activities, which translates into actions that are compatible with your true nature. Because Consciousness knows what it is that you are reaching for, it (Self) knows how to guide you from where you are to those things that are in your highest and best interest. This includes not just your intentions here and now, but also the intentions with which you came into the physical form.

While you are in the physical form, you are behind the steering wheel, but you can either steer based on the physical mind alone (which is not empowered on its own), or you can sync up to the broader knowing of Consciousness and be guided from that vantage point where the clarity of the bigger picture resides. In other words, the Self did not focus into the avatar with the idea of the avatar blindly driving around in the world, but rather for the Integrated Self to be inspired to experiences, and to listen to your Inner Guidance on how best to direct your actions.

The Subtle Guidance of the Self

The guidance that you receive in this fashion does not come with flashing neon lights and loud sound effects to get your attention, but rather comes as an idea, an inspiration, a thought, a dream, a feeling.

A *knowing*.

Each of us has a different communication style with Consciousness, and as you come to identify yours, you will get to know what to listen, look or feel for. One of the things that keeps people from experiencing this interaction is the undirected busyness of the mind. Because of the subtlety of your inner guidance, if the mind is always noisy or occupied, it is hard to sense your inner wisdom.

And it is when you ignore the subtle communication, or simply miss it because of life's never-ending stream of distractions, that you may start getting bigger signposts that the path you're on is not aligned with the path that you *truly* want to be on. For example, when your body starts giving you signs (like excessive stress, or perhaps symptoms of illness) that your current course is in opposition with what you *truly* want (well-being), that is a more emphatic but valuable sign of where you are.

As we've alluded to earlier, you can always assess how *close* you are to your Inner Peace by checking in with yourself about what is happening in your inner world. In other words, you can assess what your emotional state is. If you *feel* in close proximity to your Inner Peace, that is your confirmation, and you know that you are then able to pick up on the subtle communication and guidance of Consciousness.

Understanding Your Emotional Backdrop

As we've discovered so far, alignment is akin to a variable: in every moment of the day, you are on an emotional spectrum.

You have a *proximity* to your Inner Peace, which means you could be closer or farther from your Integrated Self. Your emotional state at any moment reveals the amount of resistance (the gap) introduced by your focus.

For example, being merely annoyed is closer to your Inner Peace (has less resistance) than when you are in a rage (which has more resistance). When there is practically no resistance, you are in resonance with your Inner Peace which feels like peace, joy and love.

These moment-to-moment emotional states form your *emotional weather*, and taken together over time, these form your average proximity to your aligned state, which we can call your *emotional climate*.

Why Does Your Emotional Climate Matter?

When you become well-versed in practising alignment, you will come to understand that there is only *this moment* over which you can exert dominion, and as such the only thing to care about in any moment is your proximity to your Inner Peace *in that very moment*. By caring about the various moments as you go, you can change your average proximity as a natural consequence.

The single most important effect of an average proximity that is closer to your Inner Peace is that you actually feel better about life on average, and that is because you will be able to look at life from a different perspective more often: the perspective of the Integrated Self. You will see the bigger picture, and be able to follow your Inner Guidance. You will know who you *truly* are.

Building a life from that basis makes for a life experience that does not feel out of control anymore. No longer will life be something that's happening *to* you, because you will understand the reason for being here, which isn't to collect as much money as you can, to please as many people as you can, to gain your family's approval, or to gain a religious leader's approval.

No, all of these things amount to "treasures on earth, where moth and rust destroy and where thieves break in and steal," as Jesus put it. These are the things of the avatar, all of which are temporary, because the avatar itself is temporary. The Self is the greater part of you, an enduring and ever-evolving stream of Consciousness that is the source of your true nature. It flows through and beyond this physical expression, and you remain connected to it whether you acknowledge it or not, and whether you believe it or not.

Another important effect of a life lived in close proximity to your Inner Peace is that many more of your moments are empowered, which means that many more of your moments put you on a road to more experiences that resonate with your true nature.

Here are some powerful examples of this:

- You may have better experiences while interacting with others because you radiate your alignment with your Inner Peace. I myself have noticed a remarkable uptick in the number of positive, rewarding interactions I have had with other people since I started this journey, even with people others have described as difficult, frustrating or otherwise problematic.

- You may have fewer health issues because you live closer to your source of peace, joy and love, and you allow the wellness that Consciousness radiates in abundance to flow *through* you.

- When unwanted things enter your experience, you don't become entangled with them by feeding them with your attention. This allows you to remain in emotional equilibrium.

Is Contrast Inevitable?

While it certainly is beneficial to your life experience to be in alignment as often as possible, because it brings your emotional climate closer to your Inner Peace, and therefore averages your experience out to a place of less resistance, the truth is that there will always be an ongoing conversation with shadow while you are in this physical form. Contrast, the interplay between Light and shadow, is simply what it means to be human; you knew it would be a part of your physical experience from before you focused down into the avatar. It's part of the reality of physical existence.

Luckily, you can always guide yourself back to your Inner Peace. When you are not fully aligned with Self, your emotional state acts as a clear signal that you've stepped away. The more frequently you connect with Self, the more quickly and easily you can return to this state.

This is really where the knowledge and understanding of your Inner Peace becomes immeasurably valuable. Even in those moments where you have stepped away from your Inner Peace, even a small step, you will *know* of your Inner Peace's existence, and the very fact that you *feel* outside of it *means that it exists.*

But even more than that, you will know how sweet it is to enter that place of Inner Peace and you will want to return to that state, which helps to motivate you to return Home—your natural state.

Above all, when you have tasted that eternal peace which "surpasses all understanding" and know that it's always there, it really adds a deep, underlying sense of comfort and hope. This is true even in moments when you have taken a fair step out of your Inner Peace. Of course, the moment that you step back in, you will be able to look at your situation from the perspective of Self, and the "earthly" problems will dissolve from this view because these are all temporary. The Self maintains a point of view that is at once broader and deeper, and which "floats above" the fleeting concerns of the avatar.

As you stabilise your perspective, you stabilise your foundation of Inner Peace, setting it as your new equilibrium.

Your Practice
Insights for Application

This chapter introduces the inward journey towards your Inner Peace, showing how alignment with Self opens access to your Creative Source and inner guidance.

Listen to Subtle Guidance

Your Self guides you from its vantage point with greater clarity on your highest and best interest. This guidance is subtle, arriving as an inspiration, a feeling or a knowing, not "flashing neon lights".

Quiet the Mind to Hear Self

The undirected "busyness of the mind" is the main obstruction to hearing your inner wisdom. Periods of stillness can help you sense your subtle guidance.

Your Body is a Sign-Post

Physical signs, like excessive stress or illness symptoms, can be early-warning signals that your current course is in opposition to your well-being.

Your Emotional Backdrop

Your emotional state in any moment reveals your proximity to Inner Peace (alignment) and the amount of resistance you are introducing.

Empower the Moment

You have power only over the present moment. Focus on your proximity to Inner Peace in this now to naturally change your overall emotional climate over time.

The Eternal Over the Temporary

The temporary things of the avatar (money, approval, status) can distract from what truly matters. The Self, that enduring and ever-evolving stream of Consciousness, is the greater part of you and the source of your true nature.

Contrast is Part of the Journey

Conflict and shadow are inevitable while you're in this physical form. Stepping away from alignment is a temporary emotional weather shift, not a moral failure. Your ability to accept *what is* will empower you to direct your emotional climate.

CHAPTER NINE

Directed Change

The Primacy of the Inner World

BECAUSE THE WORLD IS REFLECTIVE, it brings different experiences across your path based on the emotional state that you offer (broadcast) on all of the different aspects of life. While it is easier to see the link with some things than with others, most people can easily relate to being healthier and feeling better in their bodies when they are peaceful or getting tension headaches and getting sick when they are stressed. Also, think about how many fewer accidents there would be on the road if all or most of the drivers were calm, at peace and present in the moment.

What happens around you and what crosses your path is not independent of what goes on inside of you. These things are all connected. While not every external event is necessarily a direct reflection of your inner world, your reactions can give you valuable insights into what lies beneath. Ultimately, someone's relationship with external factors that entered their awareness will always be shaped by their perspective, which also forms their experience.

As you can see from the discussions so far, and those that we are yet to have, this relationship between the inner and external worlds is an important one. For now, I'm going to leave you with two quotes that contemplate this concept.

This brings to mind a teaching from the Buddha: "It is wrong to think that misfortunes come from the east or from the west; they originate within one's own mind. Therefore, it is foolish to guard against misfortunes from the external world and leave the inner mind uncontrolled."

Jesus touched on a similar idea: "You clean the outside of the cup and dish, but inside they are full of greed and self-indulgence. Blind Pharisee! First clean the inside of the cup and dish, so that the outside may become clean as well."

It is worth remembering the simple truth that you cannot change the reflection in a mirror by trying to manipulate the reflection itself. You can only change it by changing what it is that is being reflected.

Are you ready to take back control over your experience instead of giving it to the things and people in your surroundings?

Alignment before Action

For most people, desire and the response to it arise from a place of wanting to soothe the discord that they feel within them.

For example, Jane wants the corner office because she believes it would earn her the respect of others, which she expects will make her feel better about her life. What Jane doesn't realise is that what she really wants is to feel secure, valued and joyous with who and what she is.

John may want a partner because he does not want to be lonely, and he believes that he will feel more in harmony and loved if someone else helps him to feel more whole or shows him love from outside, yet what he truly wants is to realise his true nature, which *is* love, and only *then* will he be able to form a romantic relationship that resonates with that state of being.

That is to say, many kinds of desire come from a place of lacking, which is not the place from which you want to direct your life.

Conversely, in some circles, any and all desire or intention to create is seen as something to transcend, but that is not aligned with the purpose of creation, which in itself is an intention to have experiences and grow. That is the very reason behind coming into the human form in the first place: Consciousness is expanding, and *in* this form and *through* this form Self is still expanding, but it is not doing so from a place of feeling lack, or feeling broken or needing to become whole. The Self is whole but also expanding, and will always be.

The important distinction is the reason *behind* the wanting.

For example, being ready for a partner because you want to share wonderful things together is a wholly different intention than coming from a place of loneliness or a need to fill a void. The types of interpersonal relationships that result from the two different angles are complete opposites, and we will consider this distinction more in the section on relationships.

It is for this reason that it is imperative to first go inward, and then to consider what comes next. You want to sync up with your Inner Peace first, and from that place of being whole you want to consider what you want to add to your experience that resonates with the creation process of the Self. Not only is that the only way in which you will allow true joy now, without having to first obtain something external to you, it is also the way in which you are empowered to curate your life experience.

People sometimes think that to be in alignment, or self-realised, means to have *no* wants, desires or intentions for creation. There is an element of truth in that statement, but it is not as straightforward as you might think.

Perspective Matters

In the teachings of the Buddha we come across this link between desires and suffering: "Yet people do not understand this spirit of Buddha and go on suffering from the illusions and desires that arise from their ignorance." When people talk about wanting, it is important to understand from which angle they are approaching desire. A desire can be seen from either the perspective of the avatar or from the perspective of the Integrated Self. Why is this distinction so crucial?

The Avatar's Perspective: Desire as Compensation

When there is wanting solely from the perspective of the avatar, the wanting often comes from a place of feeling broken, vulnerable or insecure, and therefore the avatar looks for ways to bolster its own identity, which typically comes in the form of *needing* to change its surroundings in order to try to feel whole, secure, at peace and so on. It looks for things and people through which it hopes to enter a peaceful, loving state, and in so doing shifts the locus of control to others and the external environment.

But once you understand that the feeling of wholeness can only come from a place of integrating the mind of the avatar with the Self, and that no relationship, job or physical possession can truly provide you with a substitute for your own Inner Peace, then you can see why an Integrated Self is never found *wanting* — it does not need anything *external* to change in order to be in a state of Inner Peace. Trying to compensate for the lack of a relationship with Self is futile, even when we're talking about things that the avatar is *convinced* will soothe itself. It is then that desires arise from "ignorance", i.e. not understanding that external things cannot bring pure joy.

Pure Desire: Creating from Wholeness

Some people and philosophies see *all* desires as a cause of suffering and believe that because true integration with the Self means that you already feel whole, loved and at peace, this must also mean that you are left with no desires or intentions to co-create. While it is true that when you are looking through the eyes of the Integrated Self, you do feel whole, at peace and loved, that does not take away from the fact that you are a creative being at your core. Having that fundamental characteristic means you'll continue to *want* to expand in various ways, including creating experiences for yourself and others. Even the fact that you are here in this physical form was a *choice* (a pure desire) made by Consciousness to further experience, expand and create, and as we've established here, that does not mean that Consciousness is not whole, brimming with love, and at peace already.

It really comes down to the perspective from which you are "wanting" to create. Are you looking for something that you think will bring your Inner Peace to you, and thus attaching yourself to a physical item or outcome, or are you simply wanting to co-create as an expression of your joy, without attaching to the outcomes? In other words, are you desiring something to try to compensate for being outside of your Inner Peace, or do you already feel firmly planted in your Inner Peace and from there you wish to have certain experiences? The former is from the perspective of the avatar, and the latter from the perspective of the Integrated Self. The latter is what I refer to as a pure desire, because it does not come from a place of resistance and is in harmony with the Self.

Alignment: The Gateway to Creativity

One of the characteristics of Consciousness is that it is creative. Your body and the world that you live in are vivid expressions of that creativity. As a part of Consciousness, you are also continuously creating, whether you do so consciously (deliberately) or not. Now, some of the things that humans create are in resonance with the creative intention of Consciousness, and some of them are not. Some things are purely spinoffs of the human mind, but they are creations nonetheless. However, the creation process is vastly different when it is solely a creation from the human mind and not in resonance with Self, than when it is a co-creation between the avatar and Self. When you are co-creating with the Self, you are in the creative flow.

When you are in this creative flow, you are creating *from* your Inner Peace, as that is the state of Consciousness, your Creative Source. You are then creating from the inside out. The difference between co-creating with the Self and creating from *need* (self) lies in the experience of the journey and the ultimate impact of the creation on others. Creation in resonance with Consciousness is fulfilling and has the potential to positively impact the alignment of others, whereas creations in dissonance with your Self do not feel like expansion, growth and fulfilment, and they may negatively impact the emotional states of others.

Your thoughts influence your emotional state, i.e. they impact your proximity to your Inner Peace, and they therefore affect your degree of resonance with your Creative Source.

The Principle of Emotional Synchronicity

In order to sync your thoughts with the ideas, knowledge and wisdom of Self, you need to be in the same emotional range — the state often described as the "Kingdom of God". This reminds me of why Jesus said it is already within you: you have access to it; you just have to synchronise with it to *live* it.

But your proximity to your Inner Peace isn't a constant, it is a variable. In every moment you impact your degree of resonance with your Inner Peace and over time you can shift how close to it you are on *average*, and how frequently and for how long you have access to it. Of course, when you do not sync up with it at all, you then experience the types of emotional states which can be described as "hell on earth".

When you are far from your Inner Peace, you can tell that you are not close to your Creative Source—it is nearly impossible to be creative when you are anxious, angry or depressed. Although your Creative Source is always available to you, you will *feel* disconnected when you are emotionally far from your Inner Peace. And as your Creative Source will not change its state of being to meet you wherever you may be, you need to be the one making the adjustment to *your* state so you can once again be in resonance with Self.

We read in the Bible of how Paul the Apostle already tried to communicate the principle of adjusting your focus to be in sync with your Inner Peace when he said in Philippians: "Finally, brothers, whatever is true, whatever is honourable, whatever is right, whatever is pure, whatever is lovely, whatever is admirable—if anything is excellent or praiseworthy—think on these things. Whatever you have learned or received or heard from me, or seen in me, put it into practice. And the God of peace will be with you." The Buddha expressed a similar idea: "But if a person speaks and acts with a good mind, happiness follows him like his shadow."

The Formula for Directed Change

The process of changing or curating your experience can often feel complex and intimidating, but the truth is that the fundamental law governing your reality is elegantly simple. We can express the forces that are constantly working against each other in your experience—your pure desire for alignment and your resistance to it—as a simple formula:

Desire – Resistance = Outcome

This merely says that the outcome that unfolds in your experience is a result of both your desire and the level of resistance that you hold, and in order to change the outcome of something, i.e. to improve the experience, the resistance needs to be sufficiently low to have a positive outcome.

It is important to understand that the first and most significant outcome of this formula is your inner state. When desire is dominant, the emotional gap between you and your Inner Peace closes, and that is what you truly seek. It is really a different expression of cause and effect at play. Any framing of an outcome in the physical world is the result of many co-creative factors, but what you do have control over is your perspective, and that is where the true power of this formula sits. By shifting your perspective and softening resistance, you open yourself to what is in your best and highest interest, even if that looks different from what the avatar had in mind.

We can also think of it in a different way. If you do not change what's going on inside of you before you seek to change what's going on outside of you, and you try to change the circumstances as the disempowered avatar instead of taking empowered steps as the Integrated Self, you will most often fail at truly shifting your experience. Even in the cases where you manage to make some changes, there will be other things in your experience that make you feel the same way as you did before.

Remember, the outer world reflects the inner world, and you cannot change the inner world by changing the outer world. You will still tend to feel the same way, and therefore the essence of that emotional state will still be reflected to you by the world around you. Lasting change is an inside job!

However, sometimes a change in circumstances can be a *catalyst* for a change in your emotional climate, which will then reinforce the changed circumstances.

For example, if you are a writer and you take a week to go write somewhere in the mountains, you may find it easier to connect with your Creative Source, because your focus has shifted to be more in the current moment—you're taking in the beauty of the scenery and thinking fewer thoughts that are in opposition to your connection with your Inner Peace. In that way, an external factor has led to a shift in focus, which changed your emotional weather for that time. Whether it leads to a shift in emotional climate will depend on what you do with your focus in most of your future moments.

What often happens, though, is that as soon as the "newness" of an external factor wears off, it is less likely to keep your attention (focus), and after that point, what you *choose* to focus on is of much greater importance.

Directed Change: A Story of Two Buckets

Let's play a game to see the Experience Formula in action!

Think of a bucket labelled 'Subject X' that you're filling with rocks. Every time you think a thought specifically about Subject X, you're placing another rock in the bucket. If you're thinking that thought from a place of association with the avatar, the rock is small. When you're thinking that thought from a place of alignment with Consciousness, the rock is significantly bigger. As the bucket fills, the more you activate things in your experience that are related to Subject X.

Now, you may think "That's not fair! Doesn't it make a difference whether I think thoughts that are aligned or misaligned?"

Okay, you got me. So let's say there are two buckets for Subject X. One is green, and that is where you place all your "pure desire thought" rocks about the subject, and the other is red, where you place all your "resistant thought" rocks about the subject. All other rules remain the same, except for one new rule that will only make sense now that we've split our buckets into two colours: When you're thinking generally aligned thoughts about life (which comes naturally while you are in alignment), you're slowly sending a trickle of sand into all your green buckets across all subjects existing in your experience. Conversely, when you're thinking generally misaligned thoughts... well, I bet you can guess what happens then.

What does this tell us? The more time you spend on the misaligned thoughts, the longer it takes to fill up the bucket that you actually want to fill up. And you will feel the discord within you, because you are meaning to fill up the green bucket, but somehow it's not filling up.

In other words, your specific thoughts on a subject as well as your general thoughts, which determine your general mood (which is just your emotional climate), all make up your experience.

We can state it in terms of the Experience Formula:

Desire – Resistance = Outcome

To get a positive (wanted) outcome, the desire must be stronger than the resistance, and the inverse is true for a negative (unwanted) outcome. Limiting beliefs are contained in the Resistance component, so they can prevent a positive outcome in your experience if you allow them to dominate.

The primary challenge in minimising resistance is that the avatar genuinely believes it's being helpful. It clings to fear, doubt and worry because, from its limited perspective, these emotions are forms of protection. The avatar confuses worry with preparation. It wrongly thinks, "If I constantly worry about failure, I won't be surprised when it happens." And it holds onto guilt because it thinks that guilt prevents future mistakes. But we have to see it for what it truly is: resistance is simply the avatar's flawed, but well-intended, strategy for survival.

When something desired manifests, though, is determined by there being a sufficiently positive flow of energy to bring it to fruition, either by increasing the focus on the true desire, or by lowering the level of resistance in opposition to it. The more pure energy you can direct, the easier your experience changes in that direction. Remember that focus is the key here, and that you can either focus in ways that are aligned with who you Truly are, or that don't line up with that pure image of you. The former increases pure desire, and the latter increases resistance on the subject.

The Painter's Two Buckets

The Experience Formula is the fundamental law that governs the reality you experience every day. To understand how it works in practice, let's bring in our two buckets—the green bucket of desire and the red bucket of resistance—and watch them fill through the eyes of the painter.

The painter stands before a blank canvas.

The desire is the pure impulse to create, the wish for the profound peace and flow-state that comes from expressing beauty. This energy is a direct feed to the green bucket. Every time the painter focuses on the joy of the act, or the vision of the masterpiece, a "pure desire rock" is dropped into the green bucket.

But then, the avatar appears. This is where resistance is born. The avatar—the mind governed by fears and the need for external validation—begins its internal monologue:

"This will be compared to your last failure."

"You aren't talented enough."

"You'll never sell it."

This relentless tide of self-doubt, comparison and fear is the resistance. Every one of those limiting thoughts is a "resistant thought rock" dropped straight into the red bucket.

If the painter remains tethered to the avatar's resistance, they are constantly feeding the red bucket until the pure desire is consumed by the introduced resistance. The resulting painting may be completed (if they get that far!), but the process will be strained and absent of joy—and joy was the reason behind wanting to paint in the first place.

Conversely, if the painter recognises the avatar's voice, chooses the Integrated Self, and minimises the Resistance, they stop feeding the red bucket. They pour all their energy into the green bucket of pure desire. The result is a flow state, and the outcome radiates with the very peace, joy and love that was their initial desire, and which abundantly flowed during the creation process.

The painting itself is simply the physical evidence (an add-on) showing us which bucket, the green of alignment or the red of resistance, was winning the race in the creative process.

The Creative Flow Check

This is yet another good reason why alignment is the first order of business: because it is the prerequisite for all true creative expression. Creatives look to enter the state of flow, where their ideas and inspiration are unleashed. However, the mind cannot be cluttered in that state, and their attention is entirely focused on the moment. In this state they are at peace and the creativity is allowed to flow. This stands in stark contrast with anxious, worrying, angry, or despairing emotional states—these are not compatible with your Creative Power.

Those in the arts know the value of getting into that creative flow before or right at the moment that they intend to start the creation process. Some refer to this as getting into the zone, which is another way of saying that your focus is on the here and now without resistance being dominant.

Because of the creative nature of Consciousness, you can do a quick "gut check" on your current state of alignment by asking yourself, "would I be able to be creative the way that I feel now?" That is a shorthand technique that you can use until you become more comfortable with acknowledging whether your emotional state puts you closer or farther away from your Inner Peace.

We know that children can be creative most of the time because they are still in a place where they can let go of Resistance pretty quickly, which means that they can enter their Inner Peace fairly easily and effortlessly. Jesus echoed this principle when he said, "Truly I tell you, anyone who does not receive the kingdom of God like a little child will never enter it."

Because your proximity to your Inner Peace ("Kingdom of God") varies moment-to-moment, detachment and presence (not worrying about yesterday or tomorrow) are what allow you to enter it. These are qualities that children embody naturally, which is why they tend to be in resonance with the Self more than adults typically are.

Adults, after all, have spent a lifetime training themselves to worry, to care more about the opinion of others, and to conform to the beliefs of society, and that keeps them outside of the "Kingdom of God".

This journey of self-mastery is your opportunity to reclaim your innate power and be guided by it. It's a journey you've always been ready to begin.

YOUR PRACTICE
Insights for Application

This chapter emphasises that lasting change is an inside job, where you direct your focus and shift from reaction to empowered action.

The Primacy of the Inner World

The world acts as a mirror to your inner state. Not every image is a direct reflection of your inner world, but it gives you an overall image. Remember it is still a reflection: what you see cannot be changed by manipulating the reflection itself—only by changing what is *being* reflected.

Alignment Before Action

By syncing up with your Inner Peace first, you can consider from a place of wholeness what you want to add to your experience. Action motivated by a sense of lacking or a need to soothe inner discord is not empowered, and cannot lead to the fulfilment you are truly seeking.

Creating from Wholeness, Not Lack

Notice the reason behind your wanting. A desire to share wonderful things with a partner is a wholly different intention from a desire to fill a void of loneliness. The former is a pure desire, where you are creating from wholeness. The latter is the avatar looking for something external to compensate for a disconnection from Self.

The Experience Formula

You'll find the effect of the Experience Formula everywhere in your life: *Desire – Resistance = Outcome*
When your pure desire is dominant and resistance falls away, the outcome naturally moves in the direction you truly want: to live as the Integrated Self. Your inner state will show this change to you in real time.

Recognising Resistance

Resistance often arises from the avatar's ignorant but well-intended strategy for survival. It confuses worry with preparation and clings to fear out of a misguided desire for security. Recognising it for what it is makes it easier to choose the perspective of the Integrated Self.

The Creative Flow Check

A quick "gut check" can help gauge your alignment: "Would I be able to be creative the way that I feel now?" States like anxiety, anger or despair are incompatible with your Creative Power. Children tend to enter their creative flow easily because they are naturally present and quick to let go of resistance.

Paths to Inner Peace: Focus Aerobics

Beginning the Journey of Self-Mastery

IN ORDER TO BE IN alignment more consistently, it is helpful to understand that there are many ways to get into that aligned state, and the best way for you may be quite different from that of the person next to you, or even from what is considered to be the most popular way. Alignment is more of an art than a study of science.

Therefore, anything that you can do or give your attention to that takes you into your Inner Peace is a good way to practise your alignment, as you ultimately want your mind to allow you to return to your natural state; to be the Integrated Self. We attribute the alignment variability to the inner workings of the mind, because it is the mind that creates the illusory separation between the self (avatar mind) and the Self (eternal mind). That means that it is through the mastery of the mind that the separated self can once again become one with the Self, and this is why there are many ways to open the doors to the Integrated state; much of the journey is about finding out which ways or tools work for you to enter your Inner Peace.

For most, the knowledge of such a state is the first step towards beginning a journey of self-mastery. Not a journey in the sense of attaining something that you do not have, but rather a journey of allowing yourself to gain access to and uncover what you *already have*.

Once someone learns in some way of this Inner Peace within them, they are more likely to recognise it for what it is. Not in order to be able to name it, but as a marker or reminder to more easily return to it; a bit like calibrating a compass. Anyone who knows that they have experienced it will tell you of its sweetness and how it feels like your true home: a state of lasting joy and peace.

Once you understand what it is, once you've experienced it, you really will want to stay in and around it as much as you can, simply because you do not want to deprive yourself of it. It just feels *so much better*.

This is why the present moment is the only one that truly matters. Your power to change your life is not in yesterday's regrets or tomorrow's worries; it is solely in your choice of focus right here, right now. The moment-to-moment decision to choose alignment is the only way you can shift your overall emotional climate.

And, as we have discussed, *feeling better (that is, living as the Integrated Self),* is the itch at the back of the mind of every avatar. It is the call back to your true and natural state, and anything less will simply leave you perpetually unsatisfied and grasping at the illusory.

Why Settle the Mind?

Many of the ways to step into your Inner Peace revolve around the idea of slowing down the thoughts running through your mind. There are two main reasons for this.

Firstly, when your thoughts slow down, your mind is quieter, and as a result there is less clutter, which allows you to follow your Inner Guidance more easily. Just imagine how much easier it is to get into that inspired zone where your ideas flow freely when your mind allows there to be a quieter space, one within which the inspiration of Self can be more readily received.

Secondly, the thoughts that run through our minds are often of a nature that actively takes us away from, or keeps us away from, our aligned state. And once there are fewer thoughts, or even no thought, the "forces" that keep you from that state weaken or dissolve. The very things that pull you out of alignment are pushed to the side, allowing you to return to your Inner Peace.

It's rather easy to see why most of the "problems" in your life are purely mental constructs that do not relate to this moment. There are a lot of "what if" types of stress and anxiety-provoking thoughts. So you may lie awake at night and start thinking about "but what if this happens" or "what if that does not happen." And that is, of course, extremely tiring, because in this moment you have no power over the past or future. All your power is in *this* moment, and those kinds of thoughts do not help to empower *this* moment. As a matter of fact, those thoughts direct your creative energy to energise unwanted states and circumstances.

Similarly, people replay events in their head trying to change something that has happened in the past, but of course that is not possible because it is not happening in this moment. You cannot disempower yourself enough in this moment to change the past, but you can choose what you now *think* of the past.

But when all or most dissonant thoughts come to a halt, then you automatically start to return to a place (state) of resonance with the Self. That is to say that when you just "are" without any disempowering thoughts or thought-commentary, you naturally return to the state of your true Self, which is pure peace, joy and love.

That is why I say the Self is who you are at your core, your natural state, and you already have it within you; nothing needs to be attained or earned.

It is about you *allowing* yourself to enter that state: your *home* state, your *eternal* state.

Meditation as a Tool for Alignment

That brings us to the method people most frequently follow to access their Inner Peace, which is meditation.

The intention behind this ancient practice is to learn focus in a manner that aligns the avatar with the Self, which is *exactly* what we need for this.

Now, from what we have discussed so far, you can probably see why one of the meditation modalities is to try to settle the mind. That typically involves setting aside time where, as thoughts come into your mind, you do not attach to them, give them your focus or express commentary on them. They simply are as you are, and you simply let them pass.

With this practice, you will learn to direct your mind for longer periods at a time, maybe starting at 5 minutes and working your way up to longer intervals as you become more practised.

Meditation is not just meant as a practice for your time slots dedicated to it. The practice you gain by meditating is just that: *practice*. By applying the skills you obtain during your meditations to other moments throughout the day, you can more easily direct your thoughts when you observe them start moving in a direction away from your Inner Peace, whether due to work stress, external events or just old habits. The biggest benefit of meditation is the way it disciplines the mind. If you cannot direct your focus in a calm and controlled environment, how can you expect to do so when facing stronger thoughts and emotions?

Personally, I prefer to meditate first thing in the morning, because I feel that it helps me to direct my emotional weather for the day (which becomes my emotional climate over time). This is a way for me to already energise the emotional states that I want to have as part of my day, such as peace and love. In other words, it helps me to start my day off from a place of being empowered, which means I can better direct my thoughts in the moments that follow. It is like adding a bit of buffer to help you stay on course throughout the day.

People often think of meditation by means of the well-known "meditating Buddha" image. But if we look at how we've defined it, as something that helps you to focus in a manner that aligns you with Self, then there are many more things which can be seen as meditation.

For example, if someone is sitting and painting, this too can be a form of meditation because our painter has synced up with their Creative Power and is focused on what they are doing here and now. That is why I like to refer to these as "heart-filler" activities. These act as a way in which the thoughts in our painter's mind are settled to a sufficient degree to make space for inspiration and creativity to flow. In other words, our painter cannot be in their creative space *and* worry about something that needs to be done the next day or think about an ongoing fight with a family member. Rumination and obsession inhibit the free flow of new ideas, inspiration and creativity.

Some artists struggle to let go sufficiently of resistance-laden thoughts or thought patterns, in which case they often resort to the use of substances which *slow down* thought and thought patterns, and by reducing that resistance they then move into a place where creativity flows more easily. Ever heard of the alcoholic writer trope?

Some of these resistant thoughts and thought patterns may come from societal beliefs about worthiness, or how income should be earned, what success looks like in society, fear of failure and so forth.

But to reduce the resistance through the use of substances is, of course, a practice which holds many dangers, not the least of which is addiction and its attendant challenges, such as damage to the body and damage to one's network of friends and family.

Getting into a place of *allowing* because you have sufficiently cleaned up resistance in a natural way is not only far more sustainable, but also allows for a better life experience *overall,* and not just during the times of using the crutch of drugs or alcohol.

Similarly, people often receive ideas or inspiration while walking, washing dishes, showering or gardening. These acts engage the body just enough to distract the mind from resistance, allowing them to move closer to syncing up with their Self, which is the source of inspiration and creativity. Someone may have been pondering something for a while, but due to resistant thoughts, keep themselves from receiving the answer or inspiration. The moment that they let go a bit, the answer can come into their field of vision, so to speak. In that way, these activities can also be meditative at times, i.e. they allow the person to move in the direction of their true Self, and can even be "heart-filler" activities.

The Practice of Intentional Presence

Another common practice based on the same concept is intentionally becoming *present*. This reduces resistance by focusing your attention on the here and now, typically by focusing on yourself or things that surround you in the moment.

For example, you can focus on your breath, as it is something observable in your here and now, and by focusing on it you have just become *present*. Similarly, if you have a pet that you adore and move your attention to, you can become present by just *being* with your pet for a few moments, and recognising that same "beingness" present in your pet as in you. If you do not try to define the moment (i.e. involve the mind in that moment), you may pick up on the appreciation and love that naturally comes when you manage to look through the eyes of your Integrated Self.

The reason that focusing on the present proves effective is because most of the problems generated in people's minds are exactly that, and more importantly, *only* that. Very few of people's problems are problems that exist in the here and now. These kinds of problems often arise from looking into the past and replaying scenarios and scenes which are normally accompanied by feelings of guilt, blame, regret, grief, anger and so forth.

Of course, revisiting the past in that way and wishing that things were different is very disempowering because you cannot change any of the events from the past. All of these take you away from your Inner Peace.

Similarly, having concerns, worry and stress about future events, or events happening now but that do not impact you in this moment, has the same innate flaws as looking into the past. Most of these events are scenarios running through your mind, and the mind thinks that it can sort out potential problems if it thinks about the problem enough, which of course is *not* the case for the mind-created problems. Engaging with these kinds of thoughts only further energises the unwanted emotional states. That means that you can sit perfectly safe in your home with no threats or problems to deal with in the now, and still think yourself into a state of pure panic.

Bringing the focus to the present moment removes a great deal of these thoughts that would normally cause you to step out of your alignment.

Using Directed Focus to Shift Your State

Now, not all thoughts about the past and future have to take you away from your Inner Peace. By deliberately focusing on past experiences that bear the hallmark of an aligned state, you can help yourself focus into your Inner Peace *now*.

For example, a memory of a wonderful picnic that you had in a beautiful location with good company and delicious food can help you to return to your Inner Peace in this moment if the thoughts do not resist your true nature. It means that the memory can be used as a launchpad from which you are more likely to perpetuate that state in your next moment.

Similarly, if you daydream about something that you are passionate about, you energise the thoughts about that vision through the *now* focus that you are applying to it. By doing so, not only do you help to grow those ideas, but you also change your emotional state to be in resonance with your Inner Peace in those moments, which allows you to impact your emotional weather. That aligned state can then be used to further the project about which you were daydreaming, or it can even be applied to another subject to better your relationship and interactions with it.

The Stepping Stone Approach

The conclusion here is quite valuable: you do not have to focus on the subject that you are trying to further or to improve your relationship with in order to do so. You can use a subject that leaves you in a better emotional state before moving onto the subject you will interact with next, allowing you to approach it from a better vantage point.

Here's an example: Suppose you happen to have a difficult relationship with your mother, and there is an upcoming conversation that might be especially tough to have with her. To prepare for this discussion, you do not need to plumb the depths of your memories of your mother, hoping to find a good scrap to cling to. After all, given the energy around the thoughts about the situation with your mother, you may not have access to the perspective that the Integrated Self has of her if you jump straight onto the topic of that relationship. Instead you can choose a topic that has obvious good feelings associated with it: your painting, or your writing, or the great date you had last week — whatever it is. Use those easy-going thoughts to pull you into a happier, more peaceful state before approaching that challenging conversation, which brings your view of the person and situation closer to that of the Self. Just watch how much easier it becomes to deal with "difficult" people in your life if you first release some of your own resistance. First sync up to your Inner Peace and then interact with your surroundings.

Based on our discussion above, we can see the value in shifting our focus to the present moment. This softens the resistance that comes from thoughts relating to the past, the future and things happening elsewhere in this moment that you may focus on that have no bearing on your *now* — those "what if" and "if only" thoughts.

All of these rob you of your power in this moment. Using our directed focus, we allow ourselves to return to our Inner Peace and reclaim and empower the current and following moments.

Practising Discernment: The Attention Filter

This is an important piece to understand in practising self-mastery.

Anything you bring into your field of vision has the *potential* for you to focus on it, and you may attach to what you focus on, depending on what your thoughts are around that topic. The potential to emotionally attach to something is greater if it is something that resonates with thought patterns that you have practised before.

For example, if you know that you have lately been feeling like the world is unjust, or you feel vulnerable, or angry, and you maintain awareness of your "triggers", then you have to ask yourself whether it is a good idea to listen to the news right now, which tends to amplify those feelings in you. In other words, are you stable enough in your Inner Peace to expose yourself to something that has a high probability of activating those unwanted thoughts and feelings? If you know that it causes you to step away from your Inner Peace, what makes it worth your energy to engage in?

If you know that you are left disempowered because of your interaction with something, why would you choose to sacrifice your power in those moments where you are not applying energy in your desired direction? Especially when you are new to directing your mind, or when you know that you have active thought patterns that cause you to attach to certain experiences or subjects, it is worth considering how to lessen exposure to these things while you learn to tame the mind. And if you think about it and come to the conclusion that it seems of no value from the perspective of the

Integrated Self, then definitely consider removing it from your experience altogether.

As the Buddha put it, "A disciplined mind brings happiness." While the goal is to discipline the mind to remain in your Inner Peace regardless of what you notice, that takes practice. In the meantime, you can apply active discipline and discernment in what you expose yourself to, based on where you are on your self-mastery journey.

This is especially relevant in the information age where there are more things and people than ever to give your attention to. When you feel that you are in alignment, think about something (that you potentially want to focus on) and see whether your perspective on it changes. Is it compatible with your Inner Peace? And if not, do you want to resonate with things that do not serve or empower you?

Often people forget that this includes evaluating what you *speak* about. When you really think about it, what you *speak* about is just a further expansion of what you *think* about. Jesus expressed a similar idea: "For the mouth speaks what the heart is full of." And if what you say resonates with those you are speaking to, you really energise the subject, because now you are resonating on that topic with others, and they amplify that subject by thinking about it, reacting to it, and further activating it within themselves. The energy on a particular subject grows very quickly in such circumstances.

For example, passing judgement on people by sharing your thoughts about them with those you are speaking to, only results in further energising "being critical", not only of others but also of yourself. Jesus touched on this when he said, "Do not judge, or you will be judged. For with the same judgement you pronounce, you will be judged; and with the measure you use, it will be measured to you." He spoke of amplifying such states, and perpetuating thought patterns that determine how you perceive the world and how you are perceived. If you apply the lens of judgement, you create a perceptual loop where you see and experience the world as judgemental, thereby confirming and energising that state.

So pay attention: if the thoughts and words you are about to engage with and speak are not aligned with what you would say from your place of Inner Peace, then you know this would only further pull you away from your aligned state. This disempowers you in the moment, restricting your ability to be a clear conduit for the Light, and it can also affect those with whom you are sharing it, particularly if they are not aligned or stable in their alignment.

You Cannot Fake Alignment

How you think and speak about a subject is also important to be aware of, especially in terms of how it interacts with your proximity to your Inner Peace. If you say something but do not mean it, it is still as if you have spoken what is *truly* in your heart. In other words, you cannot trick yourself into alignment; there is no falsifying alignment to yourself.

For example, if you say something out loud about someone that you do not believe in your heart, you did not change your emotional relationship with that person or that subject just because you said something different from what you think and believe. While words can amplify the thoughts (energy) on a subject, they do not negate your actual thoughts.

Similarly, just by not speaking about something does not mean that it is not active in your mind and your experience; it is the thought and thought pattern that matters, and you can discern its essence by assessing how it *feels* relative to the emotional state of your Inner Peace.

For example, you do not have to tell someone that you are angry in order to *feel* angry. If your thoughts led you to feeling that anger, it is already active within you, and you can feel its impact on your emotional state, which is not compatible with your Inner Peace. Similarly, just verbally denying that you are angry does not change your emotional state. The underlying feeling remains until you shift your focus.

The path to your Inner Peace can take many forms, but the mind is what allows you to enter it, or keeps you away from it. Ultimately control over your proximity to your Inner Peace is dependent on the level of discipline you exert over your focus and thoughts. Our thoughts and focus are interwoven threads in the tapestry of our experience. In the next chapter we will go further into how thought curation is key in living as the Integrated Self.

Your Practice
Insights for Application

This chapter explores practical techniques for directing your focus towards alignment, from meditation and heart-filler activities to intentional presence in daily life.

Find Your Unique Path

Alignment is an art, not a science. The best way to enter Inner Peace is specific to you and may be different from the most popular methods. Anything that draws your attention into Inner Peace is a valid practice.

Settle the Mind for Guidance

Slowing down your thoughts is helpful in two ways: it creates quiet space to receive Inner Guidance (inspiration and ideas) and it weakens or dissolves the thought patterns (resistance) that keep you away from alignment.

Meditation as Discipline

Meditating in a controlled environment helps discipline the mind, making it easier to direct your focus when facing the strong thoughts and resistance of daily life.

Heart-Filler Activities

Activities like art, music, walking, or gardening can be forms of meditation. These quiet the mind just enough to make space for inspiration and creativity to flow from your Creative Power.

Intentional Presence

Intentionally becoming present (through your breath, a beloved pet, nature) reduces resistance, as most suffering is caused by mind-created problems relating to the past or future.

The Stepping Stone

You don't have to tackle a resistant topic directly. A memory or thought that easily brings you joy can help you return to your Inner Peace, so you can approach the challenge from an empowered state.

Apply Discernment to What You Let In

What you bring into your field of vision has the potential to pull you from your Inner Peace. Being aware of your triggers and choosing wisely what you expose yourself to is an act of kindness to yourself.

You Cannot Fake Alignment

Alignment is an honest relationship with yourself. Saying something you don't believe in your heart does not change your emotional state. It is the underlying perspective that matters, and your relativity to your Inner Peace will always reflect the truth back to you.

CHAPTER ELEVEN

Paths to Inner Peace: Thought Curation

SOMETIMES PEOPLE QUESTION HOW EFFECTIVE it is to try to direct your thoughts. It can seem as though thought patterns can take you to unwanted places, sometimes without you even realising it. You may even feel as though you are often at the mercy of your subconscious thoughts.

By repeatedly engaging with thoughts on a topic, your mind starts to form default thought pathways or patterns. Old thought patterns often are highly energised and have strong gravitational pulls, and can also have powerful effects on your emotional state.

Also, because these are thoughts that have been practised often and over time, people get very used to them, and usually don't expressly recognise the nature of the thoughts that they are engaging with. The mind of the avatar creates thought patterns rather quickly and easily, and these can be helpful or less helpful depending on their nature.

Even though the pull of these can become strong, you don't have to continue to recreate and deepen old thought patterns. You can change these patterns that are limiting and hold you back, i.e. those that contain resistance.

The key to making any type of adjustment to your current thought patterns is to have sufficient awareness of your thoughts and how they impact your emotional state, so that you can identify when thoughts are heading to an undirected, unwanted place. The more time that you spend in resonance with your Inner Peace, the more sensitive you will become to the difference between thoughts that support your true nature, and those that keep you outside of your Inner Peace. The good news is that it really does get easier the more you practise.

Of course, how quickly you pick up on thoughts that are not compatible with the state of the Integrated Self also determines how easy it will be to turn those thoughts around. The more a certain thought has been energised, the stronger its gravitational pull is, and the harder it will be to move your focus away from it. That's why being aware of your thoughts and your emotional state as much and as often as possible is key to mastering your mind instead of allowing your thoughts to control you.

Redirecting Thoughts

One technique that can be applied once you become aware of the unintentional direction of your engaged thought is to actively look at **shifting** your focus to **something else**—something that has less resistance than the current thought that you want to disengage with. You may recall that we discussed how there are degrees of resistance when it comes to thoughts. Different thoughts have differing degrees to which they impact your proximity to your Inner Peace. Depending on how energised the unwanted thoughts are, it can take a while to regain resonance with your Inner Peace.

The Baby Steps Approach

If an unwanted thought isn't very energised, you should be able to adjust your focus quite easily. This approach is your immediate, in-the-moment tool for escaping the momentum of a negative thought and regaining your balance. It involves finding a slightly better thought to turn your emotional state away from the current wave of resistance.

If the difference between the states of the resistant thoughts and the more positive thoughts is not too great, then it can be beneficial to direct your thoughts back to your empowered state one thought after the other. Be careful in selecting your targeted thought: if it is too far out of your current emotional range, you won't really feel resonance with your chosen replacement thoughts because you may be too far from the range in which they exist. You need a thought that is better than your current disempowering thoughts, but not *that* much better. Baby steps. As long as the replacement thought takes you in the direction of less active resistance, you will make progress in returning to your Inner Peace — even if it's by using replacement thoughts on other topics.

Imagine anxiety hits when you realise a bill is due. Instead of falling into a spiral of "I don't have enough," you acknowledge the stress, then immediately pivot: "The bill is due, and I need to address that. At least I currently have a job and a steady income that covers my needs, that can help me."

This quick, practical shift moves your energy from resistance (lack and fear) to soothing (current security), achieving a critical baby step towards a more empowered state closer to your Inner Peace.

Or let's say you had a really "bad" day at the office. Maybe you could remind yourself "not every day is this frustrating, I actually have more good than bad days at work," or "at least it is almost the weekend and then I can reset from this day." Notice that you're not going whole hog and saying "I actually love my job"; appreciation is probably too far away from your current perspective when you are annoyed with your job, so you're looking for soothing thoughts, ones that might not take you straight to your Inner Peace, but can help you change how you are looking at something currently.

The Neutral Intermediate Step

When the unwanted thoughts are quite energised, it may be easier to slow down your thoughts first or actively redirect your mind to pursue a state of neutral thought or no thought before trying to focus on higher emotional state thoughts. Doing this may be a good intermediate step in returning to your Inner Peace. For example, you can direct your thoughts to the potted plant on your desk and bring your focus to that; or to the view outside; to your breath, or a beautiful painting. These help to bring your focus back to the present if your thoughts feel like they may be running away from you a bit. It doesn't have to be glamorous, it just needs to be something non-triggering that you can focus on.

This can all come across as a little abstract, so let's look at one more example.

Maybe you've been having a stressful week. So you try to think about the weekend or something that made you smile, and you find that it just doesn't seem comforting or funny in the moment. That should tip you off that it's too much of a stretch; the emotional state of annoyance from a frustrating day has been energised enough to have a relatively strong pull on your thoughts. In this case, you could use that intermediate step where you first take your thoughts to a neutral or quiet place—think a quick meditation session or some other technique to disengage from those disempowering thoughts. Maybe you will find it helpful to take a walk outside, read a chapter of a good book, listen to your favourite song, or spend time with your favourite pet. Anything that can help you stop the runaway train for now is really beneficial.

Slowing Down Thought versus Suppressing Thought

As we've just mentioned, once you are engaging with unwanted thoughts, you can intentionally slow down your thoughts.

However, it is important to keep in mind the difference between *slowing down* thought and *suppressing* thought. When you want to let your mind become less busy, it is not about using willpower to try to keep thoughts down. Trust me, if you try to strong-arm your mind like this, there will simply continue to be more thoughts that pop up, and then you feel like you have failed at directing your mind. Directing the mind is a skill to learn and an art to master, but with practise you will see it improving and becoming easier over time.

So you want to use your focus to *guide* your mind to slow down a bit, and not simply tell it to stop thinking about something. For example, telling yourself to stop being angry or to say to your mind to stop thinking those energised thoughts of anger does not usually deactivate those thoughts. But you can guide your focus so you can become present, which will tend to help soothe a racing mind. If you guide your focus to your breath, the mind will start to slow down as you disengage with those thoughts of anger and instead focus on something that doesn't keep your mind going a hundred miles an hour. In the same way, you can guide the mind to a place of little or no engagement with thought, which is why chanting is often used in Buddhist practice as a way to lead the mind to that place of stillness.

The most important takeaway from this discussion is that denial and the refusal to acknowledge your engaged thoughts are not the same as a mind guided to a more tranquil state, and you will *feel* the difference.

The Benefits of Stillness

The first benefit of a quieter mind is that it no longer energises those unwanted thought patterns that are taking you to unwanted emotional states.

Simply slowing down the mind already brings considerable relief to many people, largely because most of the suffering they experience stems from their thoughts, including worries about the future, fear generated by "what if" scenarios, and revisiting unwanted past experiences.

That's also why the Buddha said, "More than those who hate you, more than all your enemies, an undirected mind does greater harm." When your mind is directed, it no longer runs away with those thoughts that bring forth suffering.

Stated differently, a quieter mind will make it easier to find the bridge to your Inner Peace. Once you reach a place where the mind doesn't actively keep you away from who you truly are, you naturally harmonise with the Self to live life as the *Integrated Self*.

As the Integrated Self you have access to the wisdom of Self, and a perspective of the world around you which allows the Creative Energy to flow through you in the things that you do and the actions that you take.

So far we have looked at how you can get out of the gravitational pull of unwanted thought patterns. Next, we will look at how you can weaken the gravitational pull itself so that you don't have to navigate around it by avoiding certain topics or people.

Transformative Thoughts

Transformative thinking is a process through which you deliberately change (transform) your thoughts relating to a specific topic. This is your long-term strategy, reserved for deep-seated, recurring "sticky spots" that have gained significant gravitational pull over the years. These are usually things that are energised enough that they show up frequently in your experience, and so it becomes worth your time and energy to actively change your perspective on the subject.

For example, if the subject is someone that you work with, or your current job, or a family member—really anything that you interact with on a regular basis—then you may consider looking beyond the redirection and slowing down of thoughts that we mentioned earlier.

It goes without saying that you are best equipped for this more in-depth approach when you are stable in your own alignment, because these topics are ones that are already energised and therefore have a significant gravitational pull on your focus. You do not want to be in a place where these can potentially pull you in and get even more entrenched. It's a bit like working with something that's hot out of the oven; you want to make sure that you are not touching the tray with your bare hands, so you wear your oven mitts—or in this case, a state of stable alignment.

The Process of Transformation

First, be sure to enter your Inner Peace. Take some time alone. Meditate. Do whatever it is that allows you to view the world from the perspective of the Integrated Self.

Now, to transform your thinking, ask yourself why this particular thing or this particular person has caused such an unwanted state to activate within you. By understanding what thoughts you hold that introduce the resistance, you can start to change the narrative by thinking about the subject, but from your aligned state. And from your aligned state, the way you see something or think about something is different, because that perspective is free from resistance. By revisiting the subject from your Inner Peace, you can, over time, reduce the resistance within you on the topic.

Please be mindful, though: when you are not stable in your alignment, it is easy to blame others or situations for the way that you feel, but that is not the point of the exercise. Looking outside yourself for the cause would simply further energise the thoughts that you are trying to transform. Because you know yourself and you understand what it means to be truly in control of your life, you know that you are the one ultimately responsible for your level of alignment and therefore for your emotional state. Since you also know that the world acts as a mirror that reflects your internal state back to you, you can see that as *valuable information* that you receive in this reflection process, rather than again attributing how you feel to what someone else has or hasn't done.

By doing this introspection exercise, you go on a bit of a journey inward and you can look at the situation from the viewpoint of the Integrated Self. This allows for the opportunity to reduce the gravitational pull of the thought pattern as you start activating thoughts of a higher emotional state on that subject.

Just like how you have an emotional range within which you exist, a particular subject also exists at a particular emotional range *for you*, because of your thoughts surrounding that subject. Therefore, by improving the thoughts that you have about the subject, and because you take care to view it from the perspective of the Integrated Self, you will also start to improve the emotional range in which the subject exists for you. This is how you effectively change your relationship with the topic over time. One of those changes is that you no longer blame the external factor for being a catalyst for your focus to be on thoughts of a lower emotional state.

It's important to remember that if something is really energised with a lot of lower emotional state thoughts surrounding it, it is rare that you can instantly change your relationship with it. In this case, a stepped approach can be helpful, where you continue to apply energy in a directed manner so that you change the balance of the Experience Formula:

Desire – Resistance = Outcome

As you continue to decrease the resistance and energise and purify desire, the outcome (relationship with the subject) will start to shift.

As an example, suppose you have some resistance on the subject of a family member, so much so that the mention of the person's name almost immediately activates a thought pattern which throws your alignment off balance. This is someone who comes into your experience rather frequently, and therefore the gravitational pull of your thoughts around that person cannot be easily avoided. What you want to do is *lessen* the power of resistant thoughts surrounding that person and to transform those to such an extent that it no longer pulls you away from your alignment.

Looking at the family member as the Integrated Self, you can see them for who they *truly* are, and you can put their actions and reactions into perspective. You may see their actions as stemming from a place of their own disconnection with their Self, and therefore you rather look at them with **empathy** than with anger—you *transformed* your perspective. Instead of feeling like a victim of theirs, your inner wisdom kicks in and you think about how you can best help this person to also return to their Inner Peace.

You may also ask yourself why what they do or what they say is activating resistance within you. What sore spot does it touch that takes you away from your Inner Peace? Does it feel like they are judging you, perhaps? Because even if they are judging you, if you stand securely in your Inner Peace, then their judgement really is irrelevant. In what way then does it make you feel inferior? Do you perhaps base some of your own worth on the opinion of others? Because Consciousness never questions your worth! Rather, it is from the perspective of the avatar *alone* that you do not see who you truly are.

And yes, the more you have in the past engaged with thoughts of not being good enough and worrying about the opinions of others, the more these things are going to be active in you, and the easier it will be for your thoughts around someone else's behaviour to get pulled into the gravitational field of these things within you which are already energised. That means that apart from transforming the thoughts around the family member whom you have been allowing to pull you out of alignment, you would also want to transform the thoughts around the sore point which was the initial hook upon which your thoughts got snagged.

This might look like reminding yourself more that you are worthy, you are love, you are part of Consciousness. By stepping into your worthiness more and more, the sore spot that the family member helped you notice can start to subside and therefore your relationship with them will also start to transform.

What Changes When I Transform My Thoughts?

Ultimately, by viewing a situation from the perspective of your Integrated Self, you will not only see that your reaction to the behaviour of the family member was a mirror to thoughts or thought patterns that were already active in you (otherwise it would have been irrelevant to you), but you will also see the person differently. And by keeping your thoughts about that person in resonance with the Self, the interactions you have with that person will have no choice but to change as well, because you have let the resistance that you held specifically against the person go. In terms of the Experience Formula, you have reduced the resistance and therefore it takes you to a more positive experience. In this case, it may be *better* interactions, or perhaps even *fewer* interactions, depending on the person involved and their own emotional state.

The second noticeable change is that the very thing that bothered you about your interactions with the person will start to bother you less and less. This is because the issues active within you, highlighted by your interactions with the family member, have become less energised through your shift in focus. You have weakened the gravitational pull of those things on your focus and thoughts. Additionally, because this subject is less energised, should you find your thoughts in the pull of it again, it will be easier to get out of their gravitational force, meaning you can get back into your alignment sooner and easier.

In the end, the behaviour of the family member will no longer be something to pull you out of your Inner Peace because you will have come to understand how it came about and what valuable information it shared with you—which allowed you to identify and release a pocket of resistance that was active in you. Notice how no part of this process involves changing what the *other person* does or thinks. It all revolves around changing *yourself*, and the story that you tell yourself.

Eventually you may even start to appreciate the process and how your reaction to others and situations really tell you a lot about what is active in you, and that is truly empowering.

It is worth noting that there will always be things happening in the world around you, and some of those things that you give your attention to can result in you leaving your Inner Peace. Some things may be non-recurring events, or things that have only minor impact on your alignment, and in these cases it may not be worth spending a great amount of time to understand the root of the resistance. In those instances it may be more prudent to simply realign (redirect) your focus when you notice your thoughts going off the directed path.

However, if a piece of resistance occurs frequently or it takes you so far from your Inner Peace that it takes a long time to recover from it, then it may be worth spending the time to smooth out and reduce resistance on that subject. However, if you apply the same old perspective, it does not matter how much time you spend dwelling on the past or thinking about what has happened, you cannot change it in a way that empowers you now.

For example, thinking about how you should have done things differently, said something, or should not have said something—none of this changes what was or wasn't done.

The only place where you have any power is in the current moment, and as such you can only change your *now* relationship with the past, i.e. how you perceive the past in this moment.

Beyond Positive Thinking: The Mechanics of Alignment

It is easy to mistake alignment for simple positive thinking, but the two operate on fundamentally different levels. While positive thinking often acts as a temporary coat of paint over a person's problems, alignment is the active calibration of one's focus.

The first benefit of exercising more control over your thoughts is that you can better direct how you feel, and this is because the thoughts that you engage with cause a physiological response which you can then interpret as an emotion.

Secondly, by understanding that it is your mind that is the key to your Inner Peace, you can come to have a relationship with the eternal part of you, without which there's always "something" missing. And by understanding that your thoughts not only become filters through which you see the world, but also affect your body and the things around you, you open the way to live a directed life, and also shape your world and your worldly experience.

It's important to remember that we are talking about energising empowering thoughts and de-energising disempowering thoughts, and using your focus as the control valve. It's not about ignoring those negative emotions. If you ignore the negative emotion, or merely suppress your thoughts, you do not make the necessary adjustments to your mind to have improved emotions as an effect. True self-mastery requires acknowledging your thoughts and emotions as signals that tell you which adjustments in focus are needed.

How Do I Integrate Alignment into Daily Life?

People often say that they find it difficult to find time to meditate because they are so busy, or that they get so occupied with life that they "forget" about their alignment practices and then the day derails before they realise that they have not been tending to their own emotional state. At other times they struggle to direct their mind because their thoughts are "running away" with them.

Of course, someone first needs to understand the tremendous benefit that comes with the time investment in disciplining and directing the mind. For many, they just need to taste the sweetness of their Inner Peace to want to stay close to it, and therefore set aside the time to practise directing their minds. For others, even though they know the sweetness of alignment, they get so caught up in the business of the world that they park alignment as something to get back to, and eventually further beat themselves up because they do not make the time to sync with their Whole Selves. But being in control of your life makes the small time investment worthwhile many times over.

For example, if you need to go to a place that you've never been before, is it not worth the time to either look up the route on a map or to set the GPS before you head out? Does it not make for a much better and more efficient travel experience to know where you are going and know that you are taking the appropriate steps to get there?

But even more than that, by being in alignment you are so much more empowered in every moment. That means that you are not only more clear-headed and focused, but you *feel* better. When your emotional state feels better and lighter, you are more effective at what you do. You feel so much more energised, and you have the benefit of having better "reception" of your Creative Source. You become a vehicle for Consciousness to flow through you, and that allows you to leverage the power that comes with that integrated state of being.

This is how you feel the clarity and the energy to direct your life. This is how you build your emotional house on a rock.

In the end, you do not know how long this life is offered to you, so why wait to enter your Inner Peace? Why wait to experience the fullness of Life? Choose to live empowered *now*. Do not let the busyness of life prevent you from truly Living.

YOUR PRACTICE
Insights for Application

This chapter focuses on the art of curating your thoughts, showing how awareness of unwanted patterns and gentle redirection can steadily return you to your Inner Peace.

Awareness is the Key to Change

Unwanted thought patterns can only shift once you become aware of them. More time in resonance with your Inner Peace heightens your sensitivity, making it easier to identify thoughts incompatible with the Integrated Self.

Redirect Thoughts to Less Resistance

Once you spot an unintentional, unwanted thought, shifting your focus to another subject that holds less resistance is not about denial, but about choosing what you energise.

The Baby Steps Approach

If the desired replacement thought is too far from your current emotional state, a thought that is better, but not that much better, can still move you in the direction of less active resistance. Any step in that direction constitutes progress.

The Neutral Intermediate Step

If unwanted thoughts are highly energised, taking a neutral step first (e.g., focusing on your breath or a potted plant) can slow the mind. This helps you disengage before reaching for a thought closer to your Inner Peace.

Guide, Don't Suppress

Willpower cannot suppress thoughts sustainably. Acknowledging the unwanted thought and then guiding your focus to stillness or a more positive subject allows the mind to slow naturally.

Transformative Thinking

For highly active, recurring areas of resistance (sticky spots), focused attention from the standpoint of the Integrated Self can transform your perspective on the subject, weakening the gravitational pull of the negative thought pattern over time.

The Mirror in Your Reactions

Your reactions to others often reveal what is already active within you. By viewing the situation from the perspective of the Integrated Self, you can identify and release pockets of resistance that the interaction brought to light.

Beyond Positive Thinking

Alignment is not a coat of paint over problems. It is the active calibration of your focus, acknowledging your thoughts and emotions as signals that tell you which adjustments are needed.

The Shadow Within: Understanding Resistance

What is Resistance?

IN SHORT, RESISTANCE IS ANY thought or thought pattern that takes you away from your Inner Peace. It is contradictory to the thoughts that you would have about yourself, someone or something if you were fully in alignment with your true nature in that moment. That is to say, resistance is whatever is incompatible with the perspective of the Integrated Self. Resistance disempowers you, draining your power in the current moment. It should go without saying that the more resistance you have, the less alignment you have.

For example, if you are thinking about how angry you are at someone because they "made" you feel unworthy, then that thought has resistance in it, because your true nature (your perspective of your Self) is one where there is no question about your worth. And in no way can another avatar dictate or impact how worthy you *truly* are.

How Do You Identify Resistance?

The first way to identify resistance is to become aware of when you may be activating or reactivating a thought pattern which does not *feel* like it is in resonance with the state of your Inner Peace.

As we've mentioned before, there are certain characteristic feelings that can help us identify our state of Inner Peace, such as peace, joy, love, clarity, empowerment, and so on. Any thoughts that cause you to feel in opposition to these are the first hints of the introduction of resistance.

For example, when you are thinking about how someone has wronged you in the past, and then you think about how you want to take revenge, you know that those thoughts are in opposition to your Inner Peace, as you do not feel the deep peace, love and compassion that comes with being aligned. If you were aligned and thinking of that person, you may instead have been thinking of them with compassion, knowing that this person is showing out-of-alignment behaviour because they have introduced some resistant thought patterns of their own that are preventing them from experiencing the blissful feeling of their own Inner Peace.

The Reflection of the Outer World

If you are not sufficiently aware in the moment that thoughts take you out of alignment, then over time, the resistance can show up in the reflection of the outer world.

For example, if you notice discord within yourself because of something that someone has said to you, then you know that an external experience has just indicated to you where you may have a pocket of resistance. In other words, because of your reaction to what you've observed, you can tell to what degree your thoughts and thought commentary are incompatible with your Inner Peace. Of course, if you don't recognise it as a signpost and you let your proximity to your Inner Peace be determined by what you experience in the world around you, then you react to that signpost and you further energise the unwanted thought pattern(s).

The more you react to it and focus on it, the more you will notice it in your daily life, which gives you more opportunities to react to it. This forms a cycle that can be really hard to turn around, as you become trapped in a world of continuous reaction to what is presented to you in your experience—a chain of pain.

Sometimes you may wonder how you've missed an unwanted emotional state becoming a cycle, but please be kind to yourself. If you beat yourself up about not noticing something earlier, you will just be adding further resistance, which is exactly what you *don't* want.

The trick is to accept where you are *right now*. Yes, you may not have noticed something sooner, but that was then, this is now. And in *this* moment, rather choose to be grateful for having identified the resistance, and accept the present moment, even with something unwanted in your experience. It is only through accepting *what is* that you can then better direct what you want in terms of future experiences. It starts with empowering yourself *now* by returning to your Inner Peace, so that you have the resources and understanding to adjust your course.

General vs. Specific Resistance

Resistance can show up in specific areas (such as a particular topic or person), or it can be found in a generalised manner. If someone is *generally* aligned, then resistance tends to show up more in specific areas or "pockets" of life. That is simply because as you grow in your self-mastery practice and manage to stay aligned more and more, you will tend to clean up and let go of more and more resistance, leaving only some of it behind in specific areas.

If you feel well in *general*, then resistance is not dominant in your *general* thoughts. It is often when resistance is dominant in a number of different areas that you start to feel the resistance more frequently, simply because it covers more subjects, or it may be on only a few subjects that you ponder a lot. In that way resistance begins to become generalised, i.e. when you fall outside of your Inner Peace in general.

For example, if you have a lot of resistance on the topic of your current job, then you may feel the resistance most of the time that you are at work, and because at night you think about going to work the next day, you also have the resistance active then, even if you are sitting quietly at home. In this instance, someone may describe that they feel uneasy, or anxious, or depressed in *general*.

It becomes easier to spot the area in which you have resistance if you can first align yourself with your Inner Peace by either slowing down your thoughts, so the resistance also subsides, or directing your thoughts to things that resonate with your Inner Peace. In this way, you can calibrate your emotional "instrument", so to speak, to try to stay in your place of Inner Peace and become aware of the kinds of thoughts that take you out of alignment.

If you do not notice the exact moment you step away from your Inner Peace and you find yourself wondering whether it may be a particular thought that took you out of alignment, you can increase your awareness of the nature of your thoughts and how you feel, and then put your focus on that thought. You then need to consider whether that thought resonates with your Inner Peace. If it is not a thought that is compatible with an empowered now, then you know that there is some level of resistance within that thought, or a related thought pattern that gets activated simultaneously with that thought. Of course, the more resistance is included in the thought, the further it will feel from your Inner Peace. What is key in this process is to maintain the highest level of awareness and honesty with yourself if you want to be able to evaluate your thoughts with the necessary precision.

How Can I Recognise a Resistant Thought Pattern?

Here it is helpful to look at the granularity of the resistant thought, because if you do it at a higher level, there is a greater chance of activating the resistance of subjects or aspects that roll up into the overarching subject.

For example, you may be passionate about becoming a writer. So you may think "I want to be a writer," and there is no resistance in that thought—you believe it and it leaves you in your place of Inner Peace. It feels like a thought that resonates with your Inner Peace, so you put that thought in your mental "helpful thoughts" box. Then another thought may cross your mind, like "I am good at writing", and it feels compatible with your Inner Peace, so that also goes into the "helpful thoughts" box. Now, you consider the thought "I can be financially secure as a writer," and you may feel uneasy with that thought—not because the words are not compatible with your Inner Peace, but because what you are saying and what you are truly thinking about the subject (based, perhaps, on an underlying belief) are two quite different things. So then you may dig a little deeper into that and ask yourself "Do I believe that I will be financially secure as a writer?" And if it's not a "Yes!" without hesitation, then you know that there is a sticky spot in your thought pattern about your potential financial success as a writer.

We will deal more with the softening or transformation of such a sticky spot in your thought patterns later on, but for now it's useful to know that the same topic can activate in you both assisting and hindering thoughts.

The True Indicator: How You Feel

We've seen something interesting here: you may *say* something (to yourself or others) that does not *sound* like it has resistance in it, but the way you *feel* about it is the true indicator of whether thoughts or thought patterns have resistance within them. Jesus pointed to this when he said (my emphasis added), "Truly I say to you that whoever shall say to this mountain, 'Be you taken away and be you cast into the sea,' **and shall not doubt in his heart**, but shall believe that what he says takes place, it will be done for him." In other words, just because you say something which sounds compatible with your intention, does not mean that there is no resistance on the subject. Other thoughts or thought patterns may contradict that desire, and how you truly feel about it is indicative of the level of resistance active—some of which may fly under the radar of our awareness.

In a striking demonstration of this concept, Jesus once approached his boat-bound disciples by walking on the surface of the Sea of Galilee. Peter called out to him "My Lord, tell me to come to you on the water." When Jesus did so, Peter left the boat and walked on the water, but no sooner had he left the boat than he noticed the wind and the waves, and immediately he began to sink.

Now, we can tell from this little tale that Peter knew to say the correct words, ones that showed faith and belief, but we can see from the results that he obviously still held a fair amount of resistance (doubt) surrounding his own ability to walk on water. He believed that one ought to sink into water instead of being able to walk atop it, and the external world immediately complied and reflected that belief back to him.

Of course you may also come across other thoughts where the resistance is more obvious, but when you are in the thick of things, your judgement may become impaired, making it hard to distinguish between a resistance-free (pure) thought and one that has resistance in it, i.e. in the middle of something you may lose sight of what the nature of a thought actually is. Here you can once again apply the proximity assessment to your Inner Peace.

For example, if you are angry with someone you can easily think thoughts about that person that are not in harmony with your Inner Peace perspective of that person. In that moment those thoughts feel "right" in the sense that they are in resonance with your emotional state at the time. Just because a thought doesn't feel out of place in the moment does not mean that it is resistance-free. The real question is, *does it feel out of place when measured against the state of your Inner Peace?*

We also mentioned earlier that there are degrees of resistance, i.e. there is an inverse relationship between alignment and resistance, where one thought can contain only a bit of resistance, and another a lot. That is also why I often speak of your proximity to your Inner Peace, because you can be anywhere from wholly in your Inner Peace, or fairly close to it, to very far away from it. That means that you can do a comparison between thoughts to get a sense of which has more resistance. By assessing in which emotional state a thought leaves you in comparison to your Inner Peace, you can get a sense of how much resistance is within that thought, and you can also compare thoughts to each other.

In the example of our writer of earlier, thinking "some writers do have financial success" has less resistance in it than "I might fail (financially) in my endeavours to become a writer."

This will become an important concept in our section on Thought Transformation, as it is not always easy to jump from a resistance-laden thought to a resistance-free thought, and therefore finding bridging thoughts (a stepped approach) with less resistance can be instrumental in stepping back into an empowered now.

Where Does Resistance Come From?

Of course, no one would deliberately choose to introduce resistance into their experience. It is introduced from the time that the Self focuses into the avatar form, not because it is part and parcel of the physical form, but because it is introduced through biological inclinations, traditions, societal beliefs and norms, your family, your friends, as well as the beliefs formed through your own experiences. Some of these beliefs are helpful, but others are decidedly less helpful, especially if they create thought patterns that keep you from your Inner Peace.

Because some of these beliefs have been handed down through generations and are introduced right from the womb already, we don't always recognise their impact on our lives until we start to unlock an awareness of our thoughts and where they put us in relation to our Inner Peace. Since the vast majority of people are not consciously aware of their Inner Peace, let alone have a relationship with it, living a life of alignment is definitely not typical.

Instead, we have a society in which we have normalised dysfunction, as is painfully obvious in the fact that peace, joy and clarity are not what most people feel most of the time.

In our section on the "Shackles of Society" we will delve more deeply into the beliefs that we inherit or pick up from those around us.

The Contagion of Focus

It is interesting to see how quickly someone can start to introduce resistance to a topic merely by focusing with other people, and if you do not become aware of this happening, you can go quite far down that road before ever realising that you have distanced yourself from your Inner Peace—if you ever *consciously* realise it.

For example, how normal is it for a family or friends to get together and start complaining about all the things that have gone wrong recently, discussing how poorly they are treated at work, talking about how the country has taken a turn for the worse, or saying how the world is unfair and just getting worse. And if you are not paying attention, you can be swept into the current of unconsciousness by resonating with those thoughts and ideas instead of your true nature.

That is particularly the case when you're in a group with family and friends and the conversation turns in this negative direction, because usually quite a few members of the group will simultaneously start to resonate on that level of unconscious behaviour, which makes the pull stronger. Now you have multiple people amplifying and energising that emotional state. If you're used to chiming in on these types of conversations or they have become normal to you, then you have established habits and thought patterns that may make it an easy thing to slip back into.

With these kinds of thoughts, you can tell that they contain resistance because none of these thoughts are ones that resonate with your Inner Peace. These thoughts come from anger, vulnerability and worry, and are not compatible with the perspective of the Integrated Self. In other words, these are avatar-centric thoughts that dissolve in the presence of Consciousness.

The contrast between thoughts that allow or disallow your Inner Peace also comes through in the teachings of the Buddha, which say: "It is a man's own mind, not his enemy or foe, that lures him into evil ways. The one who protects his mind from greed, anger and foolishness, is the one who enjoys real and lasting peace."

As we've said before, it is when someone associates *solely* with the avatar that they are likely to energise the kinds of thoughts that create the fear, doubt, insecurity, worry, anger and so forth, that most people walk around with. If you do not direct your mind, then it is easy to sync up with external factors such as other people or events.

It's like that saying that's become popular in self-help circles: If you don't stand for something, you'll fall for anything. If you do not have your connection to Self to guide you, you will be like a flag waving every which way, at the mercy of the wind.

And in that way, more resistance is introduced every time a situation causes you to react with thoughts that energise an unwanted emotional state—a reaction that comes from the avatar's perspective alone. That means that if you do not further direct thought, that active resistance itself leads to more resistance reflected in your experience and, conversely, when you direct your thoughts, the absence of active resistance leads to less resistance reflected in your experience. Again, the outer world is acting as a mirror to your inner world.

Similarly, by not being *aware* (of your thoughts and emotional state) during the day, you can pick up thoughts or thought patterns from someone on a subject, without meaning to do so.

For example, if someone talks about how they had so many problems with the person who renovated their kitchen, and you are not aware and present enough to see the nature of the thought and then let it go, you may start a new thought pattern, which can create an expectation for your future interactions with renovators. Just hearing it once is typically not sufficiently energising the thought pattern to be relevant in your experience too much. But say you meet with friends that evening and you tell them all about this person at work who had issues during their renovation, now your friend resonates with that idea and tells you about her sister's experience where everything was delayed for weeks. Now the thought is becoming energised enough to start creating an expectation or a belief that may be reflected to you the next time you need someone to do some work in or around your property. Don't be surprised if your next interaction with a renovator ends up with experiences that can provoke thoughts of anxiety, stress or frustration, for those states have been energised through your continued focus on it.

Why Does Negative Thinking Feel Like the Default?

It sometimes *feels* like it is easier to go down the path of negative thinking than to stay in a positive thought space.

It's not because the "dark" is stronger than the "light", or that your default place is to be in the "dark".

It comes down to *what* you've been practising in the past and for *how long* you've been practising specific thought patterns, and that more than anything else impacts where your emotional climate is. As a result, you have a natural tendency to orbit around that set point, and therefore moving in that direction happens by default if you do not maintain awareness and direct your focus. It forms a sort of *home base* for your emotional state.

It is perhaps worth mentioning here that there is no source of darkness in the same way that there is a source of Light. There is simply Light and the absence of it (i.e. shadow). Are there energy streams of the shadow? Absolutely. When humans channel their energy to thoughts of resistance, they energise thoughts that, to varying degrees, block the Light (i.e. cast a shadow). Do these form part of existence? Yes, these energy streams have been created, but they are not in close proximity to the Light.

Still, your home state remains one which is a product of the creation of the Light.

Why Do Set Points Lean Negative?

The answer, to a large extent, lies in the conditioning of society. We can see where the set point of society is just by looking at what it is that society's state seems to gravitate to. Take a look at the news and media and you will see that it tends to be more negative stories that get the most attention. As we are beings of resonance, we will always tend to resonate with something, and if we don't look to resonate with our true nature, we tend to resonate with those around us (i.e. society).

YOUR PRACTICE
Insights for Application

This chapter clarifies how resistance is formed and how to identify it as a disconnect from the Integrated Self, not as a flaw in your being.

Resistance is Misalignment

Resistance is any thought or pattern that takes you away from your Inner Peace. It is incompatible with the perspective of the Integrated Self and disempowers you in the current moment.

Identify Resistance by Emotion

The first way to spot resistance is to feel the emotional tone of a thought. Feelings in opposition to the hallmarks of Inner Peace (peace, joy, love, clarity, empowerment) indicate the presence of resistance.

The Outer World Confirms Inner Resistance

If you miss the moments you energise resistant thoughts, the resistance can show up as a "mirror" in your external world. Your reaction to an external experience (e.g., inner friction due to what someone says or does) can act as a signpost to a pocket of resistance within you. In other words, it may point to dissonance in your perspective.

Stop the Chain of Pain

Reacting to the mirror (the signpost) reinforces the unwanted thought pattern, trapping you in a cycle of continuous reaction. Accepting where you are right now releases the fight against the present moment and opens the way to regaining your power.

Examine Resistance at a Granular Level

The same topic can contain both assisting and hindering thoughts. Looking at your thoughts with greater specificity can reveal exactly where a sticky spot lies, even when the broader subject feels aligned.

The True Indicator is How You Feel

What you say and what you truly think about a subject can be two quite different things. The real measure of resistance is not in the words but in how you *feel* when you hold a thought against your Inner Peace.

The Contagion of Focus

Misaligned conversations or groups can pull you into resonance with resistance without you realising it. If you do not direct your own mind, it is easy to sync with the things in your surroundings rather than with your true nature.

Resistance is Not a Flaw

Resistance is introduced through biology, tradition, society, family and personal experience. When we don't apply our discernment, we energise patterns of resistance without realising it.

Your Emotional Set Point

Your natural state is one of peace, joy and love. But your default state depends on the emotional climate that you have been cultivating.

CHAPTER THIRTEEN

The Shadow Within: Releasing Resistance

How Do You Overcome Resistance?

SIMILAR TO PHYSICAL AILMENTS, WHEN it comes to resistance, prevention is easier than cure.

When you take into account how resistance leads to more resistance, it makes sense to limit the resistance from the start, which is the best way to limit the natural compounding effect of it. Yes, you may be aware enough to avoid energising something further, but even the awareness required to do so is sharper if you are more in sync with your Inner Peace.

Of course, you may encounter a subject that is energised from past experiences, and such subjects can quickly introduce resistance, but it is much easier to deal with things that you consider to be unwanted if you can do it from the perspective of the Integrated Self, where you have access to the wisdom and clarity that comes with being in alignment. And should you focus away from your Inner Peace because of an external factor in your experience, you can refocus a lot quicker on the types of thoughts that resonate with your Inner Peace, if that is where your emotional climate lies. That is the emotional state that you energise most often, so there is a practised thought pattern that you can leverage; a sort of gravitational pull in that direction—the "home base" that we spoke about earlier.

For example, if you are in close proximity to your Inner Peace on average, then it would feel horrible for you to be in a lower emotional state. Because it doesn't feel "normal" to you, you will make an effort to course-correct your thoughts to return to your Inner Peace. So when you are angry because of what someone has done or said, you feel emotionally out of place and you let go of those thoughts rather quickly so you can return to your Integrated perspective.

As you've hopefully come to understand by now, the compounding effect can also be your friend if you shift your emotional climate to a less resistant place. So even though you can weather the storms better in your aligned state, you also *create* fewer storms for yourself, which is a way of bringing more enjoyable experiences into your awareness.

How Do I Maintain Alignment Under Pressure?

Staying in your Inner Peace when interacting with other people, many of whom will be out of alignment at any given moment, is something that takes some practice to master. But there is more to the discussion than meets the eye, so let's start by understanding what it means if we lose our footing in these interactions.

Firstly, you are much more likely to attach to someone's behaviour when it is something that's part of a thought pattern that is active in you. It is similar in principle to paying more attention when you hear people talking about something that you are interested in—the subject is already activated because you have focused on it enough in the past that it is energised and can therefore quickly lead to a *reaction*. This reaction starts by picking up on the last thoughts and emotions that you've had on the subject.

In other words, if it was already energised before, you may find that you easily pick up a lot of that energy on the subject again. This is how people are "triggered" by things from the past, which can be brought into their experience without it having to be a recent event at all. This is often the case with traumatic events; because they get so much focus time even after the experience, they remain active and become highly energised, even when that past event might have no other impact on the present moment at all.

Of course, once you have been triggered by something, it becomes harder to get out of its gravitational pull the more your focus stays there, but the sooner you can "course correct" the better.

The Power of Acceptance

Sometimes you may find yourself caught in the gravitational pull, farther down an unwanted thought path than you'd want to be. This makes it harder to turn it around. However, by being aware that you have stepped out of your alignment and simply accepting it, without judgement, you already soften its effect just by allowing it to be. It feels less like you are on a runaway train, because you stepped back into the control room and you're looking at the gauges and accepting what they are telling you in this moment.

When people learning to tame their minds notice they've stepped out of alignment, they sometimes chastise themselves instead of simply accepting and acknowledging the emotional state. This only further energises the unwanted state because you are doubling down on the fight against the present moment. *Acceptance* of where you are is the key to letting go of sufficient resistance to become re-empowered.

Three Ways to Avoid Being Pulled In

Here are the three ways to avoid getting "pulled in" to resistance:

1. You can avoid getting into its range in the first place. For example, if you know that you get triggered by a certain person, show, event and so on, you might stay clear of that specific trigger if you can. Just remember that depending on how widespread the resistant thought pattern is, the resistance may show up in other areas or aspects of your life. If you think that you are leaving a job or a relationship because it leaves you outside of your Inner Peace, turn your focus inward to understand whether you are leaving because of something specific to the job or person, or because you haven't yet cleared up some other resistant thought pattern(s) that you will carry with you wherever you go.

2. You have to weaken the pulling force of it sufficiently so that it cannot pull you in, *or* have enough momentum to fly straight by without being pulled into its orbit. This can mean that you spend the time to clear up the resistant thoughts about it until its "pull" weakens, or it may be

that you build up so much momentum in your good-feeling state that you are not thrown off-course by what enters your awareness. In order to do so, you can do things which amplify your aligned state before you face the situation, such as engaging in "heart-filler" activities like meditating, spending time to look at the situation (and the people involved) through the eyes of Self, or going for a run—really anything that you can do to get your aligned state as solid as possible. The benefit of spending time looking at the situation from your aligned state is that you also start to build better expectations of the interaction, which will help to shift your perspective and how you feel about the situation or the people, even if your surroundings don't change.

3. Course correct. If you cannot avoid the pull for now, and you haven't weakened the pull force yet, then you have to do a lot of small course corrections to safely navigate through its pull. This requires a lot of awareness, of course, because it requires you to be finely tuned to your emotional state and to make course adjustments to your focus as you go through this particular part of your journey. That looks different for each person, and will involve drawing on the different alignment techniques that we have discussed. For example, if you were in a situation where you were flying close enough to something to feel its pull, and it is something that you cannot avoid for now, such as an interaction with a family member, or a colleague, or a supervisor, then you would want to be keenly aware of the emotional state in the moment, and when you notice that you are stepping out of your Inner Peace, you want to apply a thought-

adjustment technique to realign with your true nature. This may look like taking a walk outside, going to meditate, focusing on your breath and so forth, in order to make a course-correction before you get wholly pulled in and entangled with the subject emotionally at the cost of your alignment.

Remember that *how you feel* about a subject, and therefore what you come to expect of it, *influences* the actual interaction a great deal, especially if it is done with consistency over time. So what you *think* about a situation (and consequently how you feel about it) is extremely important.

Of course, you would also want to do whatever you can to maintain your alignment for as long as possible after you've built it up beforehand. This may involve limiting the amount of "exposure" time that you allow in a single stretch; for example, you may decide that for each hour that you are in this situation you will take 5 minutes to do an alignment adjustment, where you specifically direct (or redirect, as the case may be) your thoughts in a way to keep, or improve, your proximity to your Inner Peace. This will look different for each person, but it can include softening your focus for 5 minutes. You can become present for those moments by observing things around you which aren't triggers, like looking out the window at a tree outside, petting your cat, looking at a beautiful picture, focusing on a particular colour or sound, or concentrating on your breathing. All of these help you to become mindful and just be present in the current moment, and perhaps even to appreciate it.

As I've mentioned earlier, it is also extremely helpful to maintain a level of awareness as you go through the situation, because the sooner that you notice that you might be losing your balance, the easier it is to make an adjustment so as not to energise the deviation further.

For example, if things are going off the rails in a meeting and you see a lot of out-of-alignment behaviour around you, it is good to try to look at the situation through the eyes of Self before your mind attaches to the behaviour and you resonate with it instead of with your Inner Peace.

Undoing Disruptive Thought Patterns

What perpetuates those unwanted emotional states more than most would consciously mean to, is that we don't typically learn to direct our thoughts from a young age. That emotional climate then impacts what you see in the world around you, and then you react to that once more, which reinforces that worldview even further, often in an endless back-and-forth resonance. That is how these thought patterns become engraved on your mind.

But here's the good news: you can change your emotional climate, which changes the types of thoughts that easily come to you.

It all starts with changing and directing your thoughts in this moment, and the next, and the next, which eventually builds into a fundamental change in your thought patterns.

Being a Beacon of Light

Suppose you've become well practised in your alignment, and an obstacle presents itself on the way. By remaining aligned to your true nature in the face of this obstacle, you put yourself in the best position to deal with it, because you retain access to the wisdom, inspirations and answers from the Self: your Inner Guidance.

You will also react differently to an obstacle while you are in alignment, and you'll have the opportunity to change your relationship with things of that nature, or at the very least not further energise such things, and will therefore be able to impact the future encounters with similar things.

For example, if someone in the family is dealing with emotional distress and they come to interact with you, but you are firmly in your Inner Peace, then instead of joining them in their distress, you can be a light to them—a beacon to their natural (true) state. It is interesting to witness the typical human manner in approaching others' moments of darkness, which is almost always to *dim your own light* and join them in their distress, while what the other person **really** needs is to return to their natural state. That is what happens when you resonate by default with others—no matter where they are, emotionally speaking—instead of resonating with the peace, love and stability of Self.

You can only be a beacon of light to others if you stand firmly as the Integrated Self. That is the only way to help others find their way back to their own light.

The teachings of the Buddha feel particularly relevant here in maintaining your own light: "One should control both the mind and body, and guard the gates of one's five senses. One should be afraid of even a trifling evil and, from moment to moment, should endeavour to practise only good deeds."

Once you have become familiar with self-mastery and with how you have power over your experience here, then even in times when you notice that you have attached emotionally to something that you do not like in an experience or a person, you will understand your current state relative to your Inner Peace and will be able to guide your mind back to your true state.

It is not always easy to know where you may have an energised thought pattern that does not serve you, but if you remain aware of your emotional state, you can tell rather easily when you attach to something unwanted emotionally. By being aware in this way, you have a wonderful opportunity to use emotional waypoints to let you know early on that you do not wish to continue down a certain path. This allows you to avoid further energising that unwanted thought pattern by redirecting your focus early on. If it is something that comes up rather often, then you may want to spend the time when you are stable enough to soften the pull of the thought pattern, until such time as it no longer causes you to attach emotionally.

Undoing Creations of Resistance

Have you ever had a tension headache that just added more stress to your life? When something unwanted has come into your experience and has taken hold, it is understandable that you would want to be rid of it as soon as possible. But quite often that leads to a situation where someone does not accept where they are. In other words, they look at the unwanted and that becomes the dominant point of focus. Whether you wish for more of something or less of something, the more you focus on it, the more you energise it. Focusing on the unwanted is in itself the resistance to the wanted, i.e. it increases the resistance in our Experience Formula (*Desire* −

Resistance = Outcome), which takes you further away from your pure desire. In this case, it may be to feel at ease.

That feels counter-intuitive at times, because society or the avatar mind tells you to focus on the problem, and then somehow that should solve the issue. But this is how a compulsive thinking pattern can start. You notice something that you do not want in your experience, and then through your sharp focus on that topic, it gets energised very quickly, and as a result you start to create a strong gravitational pull around it, and eventually your thoughts start to orbit around it, and your experience gets shaped by it.

I have personally experienced the wonderful freedom from compulsive thinking that comes with taming the mind. My obsessive-compulsive tendencies eased once I discovered the freedom within. This freedom was always there, but I just did not know how to uncover it simply because I was not *aware* of its existence. Yes, I would stumble into it on occasion, but I never knew that I could *actively* allow peace, joy and clarity; I thought that the conditions around me needed to be a certain way in order for me to do so, and in trying to control the conditions around me, the obsessive behaviour and thought took hold.

It's important to know that your focus is not stagnant and therefore the energy that you apply is also not stagnant, in the same way that the focus of Consciousness is never stagnant and always expanding.

What that means is that everything that you experience in the current moment is a result of the past and present application of energy. You can apply energy in the current moment to change that which is in this moment, but in order to change what is, you cannot focus on (or apply energy to) what *is*—that just *sustains* what is. In order to have a different outcome, you need to apply the energy differently in this moment, and the next, and the next. Jesus touched on this when he said, "Therefore I tell you, whatever you ask for in prayer, believe that you have received it, and it will be yours." The emphasis is on thinking about a different outcome in this now. You have to believe that you *have received it*, and then the outcome will change. You apply your energy (focus) differently in this now to bring forth the change that you are looking to realise. In short, you cannot stand in resistance to what is, and intently focus on what is, *and* expect the conditions around you to change.

In that way, your current experience contains much valuable information, because it gives you an idea of the emotional climate and emotional weather that you have been cultivating. In other words, it has the potential to give you insight into how you have been applying your focus in the past, which resulted in something being in your experience now.

For example, let's say that you have not been paying much attention to your emotional state recently, and as such your awareness of your proximity to your Inner Peace hasn't been on point. Now you start noticing that you are having more tension headaches, which is a more emphatic indicator that your emotional state has not been quite where you would like it to be. So if you missed the signpost that would have come from awareness, you are shown a reflection of your inner world, where you can make the decision to not energise that state further. And from our earlier discussion about changing what is, it is quite easy to see how additional focus on the tension headache would not change it. Yes, you can take painkillers in the meantime to give some relief, but if you don't address how you've been focusing, then the headaches will just pop up again, in the same form or another that is similar in essence, and energise that state even further.

So let's say that the types of thoughts that you've been focusing on cause you to worry. By energising a state of worrying, things that resonate with that state are highlighted in your experience. It may include headaches, but it can also include insomnia, or finding more thoughts and things to be worried about, such as through conversations with friends or family, or being drawn to that type of news and social media content. In other words, it can be helpful to watch out for the *types* of things that have been happening in your experience, as they may all be shoots coming from the same root.

As such, my primary focus would not be on how to remove something from my experience in the shortest amount of time, but to understand where I can solidify my own alignment, and make the necessary adjustments to my focus *now* which allows my experience and outer world to evolve with that changed inner (emotional) state.

YOUR PRACTICE
Insights for Application

This chapter provides practical strategies for softening active resistance, emphasising that prevention and self-acceptance are the keys to uncovering your Inner Peace.

Prevention is the Easiest Path

Your emotional climate acts as your "home base", and when this base is close to your Inner Peace, you naturally course-correct more quickly. Limiting resistance from the start is always easier than undoing it later.

The Power of Acceptance

Acknowledging and accepting your emotional state without judgement already softens its effect. It is the key to letting go of sufficient resistance to become re-empowered, as it prevents you from doubling down on fighting the present moment. You cannot stand in non-acceptance of anything and be in your Inner Peace.

Three Ways to Avoid Being Pulled In

Three strategies can help when facing a persistent or difficult source of resistance:

- **Avoid the Range.** Staying clear of known triggers (people, shows, events) that activate strong resistant thought patterns, where possible.
- **Weaken the Pull.** Building momentum in your aligned state before interacting with a challenging situation means you are less likely to be thrown off-course.
- **Course Correct.** If you cannot avoid the pull, maintaining keen awareness of your emotional state and applying thought-adjustment techniques (like focusing on your breath) in the moment can help realign your focus.

Be a Beacon of Light

Standing firmly in your Inner Peace when interacting with someone out of alignment offers compassion without sacrificing your own power. Your alignment can be a beacon that assists others back towards their own natural state.

Your Experience is Information

What shows up in your life offers valuable information about the emotional climate you have been cultivating. Patterns in your experience, even seemingly unrelated ones, may all be shoots coming from the same root.

Releasing Creations of Resistance

Focusing on an unwanted outcome only energises resistance further. You cannot stand in resistance to *what is* and expect your experience to change. Applying your focus and energy in the now moment is what brings forth the change you are looking to realise.

You Can Change Your Emotional Climate

We are not typically taught to direct our thoughts from a young age, which is how disruptive patterns become engraved. But the emotional climate can shift, one moment of directed thought at a time.

PART FOUR

Shackles of Society

CHAPTER FOURTEEN

Unveiling the Shackles of Society

As part of our discussion on resistance, we have already considered some of the things which may lead to the introduction of resistance into our experiences. One of these is the limiting beliefs we adopt from those around us, right from the very start in the womb.

When I speak of a belief here, I am talking about a thought pattern that has been established and energised within the mind of the avatar. It's something active within the avatar, possessing sufficient gravitational pull to draw other thoughts and ideas towards it. That is why it can also be seen as a filter on your worldview, as everything that you perceive passes through your beliefs and changes the way you interpret what you take in. Similarly, the thoughts that come up in your mind often originate from active, well-established thought patterns, which is also where the mind-commentary comes from when you interpret what you perceive or think about.

This filter on your worldview can be thought of as a limiting belief if the belief takes away your creative power, which can also cause you to feel emotional discord within. Ultimately, your beliefs create your reality, and in this way a limiting belief can constrict and warp your experience.

For example, you may have a mental belief system which says that abundance can only come to you after you've sacrificed yourself for a job, and indeed that will then be your experience. Or you may believe that money will bring you happiness which limits your ability to experience joy in this moment if you do not have it. You falsely believe that lasting peace and joy will come through your surroundings, but even if the money arrives, it cannot replace the joy and peace that comes from allowing your true nature to shine through.

How Do I Identify a Limiting Belief?

At the root of any limiting belief is the inclusion of *resistance* — to your full creative power and your true nature — within that thought pattern. As such, a limiting belief will hold the same characteristics as any other thought that has resistance in it. You can tell whether a belief is limiting by assessing the degree to which it resonates with your Inner Peace and whether it leaves you empowered or not.

Does it feel in harmony with your Inner Peace? Would the same thought arise when you are steadfast and certain that you are synced up with your Inner Peace?

If the resulting emotional state of the thought is incompatible with the emotional state of your Inner Peace, then you know that there is *some* resistance within that thought, which moves you away from your Inner Peace and is resisting your full integration with your *true* nature.

Limiting beliefs, as a form of resistance, can of course crop up on any topic. Depending on what you have adopted, and from whom, these beliefs can impact the type of romantic partner that you attract (or not), the career that you enter (if any), how you see other people and interact with them, your relationship with money, and pretty much every other aspect of your life.

The Three Spheres of Influence

Some thought pathways are inherent to the human body, part of its physical make-up and tied to the survival of the species and the avatar's physical needs for self-maintenance. These include things like your appetite and other biological drives, as well as your instincts and so forth.

On top of that base layer, you introduce the beliefs that come from your own experiences as well as the beliefs held by other people. How it is introduced into your experience by those around you can roughly be divided into three spheres of influence.

The Immediate Circle

First you have the influence of your parents or caretakers, and your immediate family when you were young, stretching from your formative years to possibly today still. Especially in your very early years, you are extra receptive to new things and ideas, which is great because it allows you to learn all sorts of new skills so quickly, including speaking new languages, riding a bike, and all kinds of useful things. And because you learn these things from your caretakers, you naturally also place a great deal of trust in them and adopt most of the things that they share with you, including their beliefs. Some of these are really helpful and will serve you a great deal, and others may be less helpful. Nana might have taught you how to count and share with others, but maybe she also taught you to feel ashamed of your body.

That immediate influence later starts to expand to your **friends** as well, as they start to play a bigger role in your experience. This further extends to your **colleagues** later in life, especially on the subject of career, but you can adopt these beliefs from any person on any subject. As a general rule of thumb, the older you are when something is introduced into your experience, the less likely you are to adopt the belief, especially if it contradicts a belief which has formed part of the avatar's identity for quite a long time. The reason is obvious: old beliefs have been energised for a long time, and these thought patterns have been practised for so long that they have created a strong gravitational pull.

The Institutional Level

The second sphere of influence is at the **institutional level**. Here the thoughts of those in authority are directed at the members of their community. Even from an early age these ideas, thoughts and beliefs are shared with you. If you went to church from an early age, you would have had the experience of people, as part of an institution, sharing their religious beliefs with you. Similarly while you were at school, the ideas of the government, the educational system, the particular school, and the specific teachers were shared with you. Some of the beliefs of one institution may have occasionally contradicted those of another and you may have had to decide what was best for you, but for the most part, if you spent a lot of time in the same country or region (like most people do growing up), the different institutions would have tended to reinforce each other's beliefs.

For example, you may have gone to a Christian school where similar ideas would have been shared with you as when you went to church. Similarly, the government shares its beliefs through the rules, guidelines and laws that it makes, but also through the messaging in the media, its behaviour that you can observe, as well as through your interactions with it and its various institutions (like public schooling and the legal system). Later in life you may also come into contact with other institutions and their beliefs, such as universities, your neighbourhood's body corporate, the country club society, the company where you work and so forth. Each group of people getting together has its own collective persona, and through your interactions with them, you may or may not introduce more beliefs into your experience, and possibly even change some of your current beliefs.

The Global Level

The third sphere of influence relates to the world on a more **global** scale. Where your immediate family and institutional influences tend to have more in-person and geographically specific influence, the broader sphere is location-independent, and the extent to which it influences you varies greatly. In this bucket we have media, entertainment and social media, which tend to have a wider reach. Before the rise of the internet, this aspect of cultural sharing was a lot more limited, and therefore its influence tended to be less. At that point it may have included primarily printed media and movies, where now it includes all of that plus so much more through all of the social media platforms and the world wide web as a whole.

While traditional media was largely a one-way flow, now you can actively participate by contributing to discussions and output. As you can imagine, that provides for a lot more opportunity to energise a topic, because you are actively engaging in it, with the option of keeping it active in your focus for so much longer. Many of the social media platforms also actively encourage people to judge what is being shared in the form of like/dislike buttons and comment sections, and to look at what enters their awareness through a lens of finding things to resist and fight against. Any time you resist something, you choose resonance with that disempowering thought commentary instead of resonance with Inner Peace.

People are able to come together on a specific subject like never before and pour energy into it *together*, really energising it. Now, if you feel angry, you can join hordes of other people online who will resonate with you and amplify that emotional state. In other words, there is unprecedented momentum on topics spanning the entire globe.

Not only is there the aspect of resonance with others on a topic, but there is also the matter of ideas and beliefs which reach a lot further. Where entertainment and printed media tended to still be indirect influence in a sense, and because the interaction with it was in discrete intervals, there tended to be less focus on one specific subject. Nowadays you can seek out in very specific details what you want to resonate with, and you can have nearly unlimited amounts of interaction on that topic; and because of the clever social media algorithms, you also get presented with more and more information on the topics that are already active in your mind.

And so the beliefs of others across the globe have the potential to impact your own set of beliefs like never before—which can be beneficial or not. This depends on the types of things that you choose resonance with. Technology has made it easier than ever before to bring things, ideas and beliefs into your experience, which can have just as big of an influence, if not bigger, as those in your immediate influence circle, because you can draw things from the outside closer to you and deeper into your experience than ever before.

Depending on your emotional climate, it can either be the best of times or the worst of times; it's really up to you. You can choose to energise emotional states which are in resonance with your Inner Peace, or you can choose to resonate with and energise things out of tune with it. Luckily you don't have to rid the world of all things that do not serve you in order for you to enter your Inner Peace. You simply have to apply *discernment* in terms of the thoughts, ideas and people that you allow to have an impact on your mind and therefore your proximity to your Inner Peace.

CHAPTER FIFTEEN

Decoding the Media

IN OUR INTRODUCTION TO LIMITING beliefs, we touched on the impact that the media can have on someone's beliefs. In this section we will delve a little deeper into the "silent killers", those that are less obvious than social media because they have been around for longer, such as television, films, news and marketing.

What makes these more stealthy is the fact that the information flows in one direction—from the broadcaster to you—which can lead to you picking up certain thought patterns without you expressly knowing you are doing so. This is especially true in the circumstances where you are not aware of:

- what you are giving your attention to (and therefore letting into your experience), and

- the *reaction* that it evokes from you.

Because of the extremely wide variety of things that you can tune into in these formats, we will only look at a few examples of how this may impact your emotional state and thoughts, and consider these against the concepts of your Inner Peace and being empowered.

News & Advertising

The news is one of the forms of media where it is rather easy to see the type of influence that it can have on your proximity to your Inner Peace. The simple reason for this is that most people have extremely practised mental pathways leading them to the emotional states that are amplified by the news. These include emotional states such as anger, worry and victimhood. Most people include these states in their emotional climate, and can therefore readily resonate with what the news has to offer. That's why it makes sense that the news leans in the direction that it does, as the news publishers maximise revenue by resonating with as many people as they can, which happens most at the lower emotional states. It's basic demand and supply.

Of course, it is possible to notice the news and not attach to it, and thereby remain in your place of Inner Peace, but that requires a keen awareness of your thoughts, so as not to go down a path that you do not wish to follow. I would suggest *very cautiously* approaching the news, if you consume it at all, especially if it is early in the morning and you are trying to set up your trajectory for the day.

Similarly, a lot of the marketing in the world is based on the same principle, as those wanting to reach the masses will play to those thought patterns that resonate with most of the potential customers, which is very often in the lower emotional states.

For example, you may come across an ad on TV or the radio playing to people's worries and fears in an attempt to catch their attention and use the misalignment of the masses to their advantage.

Why Do People Cling to the News?

It is a misconception that misalignment must be constant to be impactful. Instead, it is the practised patterns of thought that keep these states active in our lives. Because most people do not focus with precision, they easily include those states, like worry and fear, in their emotional climate. In other words, they do not have to have these feelings *all* of the time, but most people have practised thought patterns that activate those emotional states enough to be quite active in their experiences. And because people tend to react to their surroundings, one person's misalignment or emotional hook, like with an advertiser, can spread quite far, like a fire through dry grass.

It is interesting to note how often people almost get anxious when you mention the prospect of parting with a regular news routine, whether it be from a printed newspaper, an online news site, someone that they follow or watch or listen to on a platform, or a podcast, or even the gossip at work. These can easily become habits, and eventually become a fix that people "need" because it gives them an opportunity to perhaps resonate with others on a particular subject. Or it may be a form of distracting themselves from what's happening in their lives in this moment, or it may even be a way to feel better, albeit temporarily, about their own life because their lives seem better in comparison to the worst things that are going on in the world, or to feel that they are not alone in their lower emotional state because the world seems to be in such a state as well. We naturally seek out resonance, but resonance with others should not come at the cost of resonance with Self.

It is very seldom that the news actually has information that directly impacts your life. Furthermore, once you start to realise that *you* are the one in control of your experience, you also realise that directing your focus and empowering your now is *so* much more powerful and relevant to your actual life experience than just absorbing the information around you. And once you treasure that focus, because you know that is what puts you either on a path directed by *you* or a path where others choose the direction *for* you, then you become a lot less willing to just give it away.

Television

In the conversation on television, we are talking about TV shows and movies, and how we may pick up or reinforce limiting societal beliefs from them.

The vast majority of shows depict a dysfunctional world, with dysfunctional personal relationships, families and relationships with material things and careers. And I'm not saying that it is not an accurate depiction of the state of a lot of the people in the world, but rather that it does energise and "normalise" those emotional states of people that resonate with the drama being shown. It's really as simple as being aware of whether what you are watching is helping to empower you in this moment or not.

Furthermore, movies and TV shows teach people to behave in certain ways. Not by themselves, of course—you can learn behaviour from those around you too. But these shows and movies can further energise or introduce behaviour which is seen as the norm in society. Again, I'm not saying that all learned behaviour is limiting, but some is.

For example, the TV often shows how people are simply reacting to the situations and the people around them. They are absolutely at the mercy of their external conditions, and that is definitely not so far off from how people react every day, but by seeing it frequently playing out on an exaggerated level only further demonstrates to people what "normal society" looks like, and *that* is what people sync up with — the "normal" (read: usually pretty negative and disempowering) behaviour and thought patterns of society.

A further impact of television is to give a distorted view of how the world actually works. For example, it very rarely links someone's external view to what is going on in their inner world, and that is because that link is not seen and understood by the majority of the world.

Another skewed representation of the world is how people's happiness is typically shown to be dependent on external factors. For example, the characters react to the story's events and by default head to the lower emotional states of anger or victimhood because of what someone else says or does; characters are hardly ever shown to take responsibility for their emotional states or direct their thoughts. TV people are essentially open targets who are at the mercy of the people and circumstances around them.

That, or the characters are unhappy until they meet the love of their life, or until they get the big promotion, or until they move to their dream house, which, of course, is the avatar's attempt at creating fulfilment. This kind of structure may be dramatically sound, but can be spiritually misleading if you're not paying attention.

Your Inner Guidance will confirm to you, so you recognise it as being true, that lasting joy is already within you and is *allowed*, not obtained or created by external means.

The Myth of External Happiness

Heart-filler or Time-filler?

Also worth considering when it comes to the use of entertainment, is whether you are actually using it as a form of entertainment for the fun of it, or whether you are using it to perhaps mask unwanted emotional weather. In other words, are you watching something because you *enjoy* it, or is it a way to cover the unease that you feel because you do not enter your own state of Inner Peace?

Entertainment can be a good way to distract yourself from an active unwanted thought pattern if it is acute, but if it is more chronic, you may want to ask yourself why this pattern is repeating in your experience. Is this entertainment habit merely a time-filler which is a way not to accept (escape from) *what is* in this moment? That's how a lot of addictions or chronic behaviour start: people are unhappy with where they find themselves emotionally and then start to turn to crutches just to feel better. This happens especially easily if you associate only with the avatar, because then you do not know to go inward, so you end up looking at the things and people around you to provide you with the happiness that you are seeking.

Unpacking a Powerful Childhood Myth

Does the phrase "happily ever after" ring any bells? That comes from all the most well-known children's books. And what harm can there be in those innocent tales, you may wonder? Well, let's have a look.

What we are shown in many fairy tales is a person who is wanting and looking for more. They are in a place of lack, and that is normally presented as the main characters being victims to forces external to them, evil antagonists that are "out to get them". And then the road to happiness for them is to find a way to change the external forces impacting their lives, and once that happens, they can reach a place of "lasting happiness". As soon as they have reached "true happiness", that happiness is theirs "for ever after".

Let's unpack this a bit then, and see what "shackles of society" we may be adopting and sharing without even realising it.

Firstly, fairy tale characters often have no control over their lives. They seem to be at the mercy of all manner of evil stepmothers and witches and curses, and there is seldom an internal shift that takes place in order for the world around them to respond (reflect) differently to them. Instead, another external force normally needs to intervene in order to change the external circumstances for them. Cinderella needs the Fairy Godmother to magic everything to perfection, because she "needs" an intervention to have her situation changed in order for her to experience joy.

Secondly, the characters normally find something that they really long for, and are convinced that once they have that, they will reach a place of eternal happiness; "happily ever after." How does that stack up against the way the universe works?

We know by now that true, everlasting joy cannot be found outside yourself. Yes, you can find things that make you feel happy (pleasure) for a few moments, but ongoing, lasting joy is an inside job. We can all relate to this. We have all at one time thought that if we could only obtain X or achieve Y, we'd be happy, and to be fair, such things and achievements *can* provide temporary pleasure when they are realised. But you probably know from experience that that sort of happiness soon starts to fade, requiring us to seek another goal, another target.

Fairy tales are meant to be simple stories for kids, and so they only tell half the story. As children, we internalise a lot of these lessons, and they become lifelong companions.

Partially because of "happily ever after", most people are on an everlasting chase, a perpetual state of running after something that they *think* will be the key to their happiness.

Yes, you will always be expanding and looking for new experiences—that is at your very core, the very reason that you are here in this form. But if you are looking at these experiences as a way to bring you everlasting joy, then you are on a road leading to nowhere. You will not find that destination down that path, despite how it may be portrayed in the media.

The good news is that you already have the keys to everlasting peace and everlasting joy. You simply have to acknowledge it and enter (allow). That place is already within you, and you are never without it. You simply *decide, through the application of your focus,* whether you will enter it or not. You don't need a fairy godmother or a charming prince to bestow lasting joy on you.

YOUR PRACTICE
Insights for Application

This chapter addresses the silent, one-way flow of information from media sources and provides a framework for using discernment to guard your emotional state.

Discern What You Consume

Being highly aware of what you are giving your attention to matters, as media easily reinforces established, non-aligned thought patterns like anger, worry and victimhood.

Be Wary of the News Cycle

The news is worth approaching very cautiously, especially when setting your trajectory for the day.

Guard Your Focus

Your focus determines whether you are on a path directed by you or a path where others choose the direction for you. Giving away your focus to gossip, anxiety-inducing headlines or advertising is giving away your power.

Evaluate Entertainment

It is worth asking whether a movie or TV show is a heart-filler (something you enjoy) or a time-filler (a way to mask unwanted emotional weather). Content that only amplifies and normalises dysfunctional behaviour may not serve your alignment.

Challenge the Myth of External Happiness

The "happily ever after" narrative teaches that lasting joy comes from changing your surroundings. Joy is an inside job that you allow, not something you obtain.

CHAPTER SIXTEEN

The Influence of Family and Institutions

FROM OUR DISCUSSION SO FAR, it's clear that family plays a fundamental role in the way that you see and understand the world, as they share with you their thought patterns from even before you were born. Because of the strong influence from the start, it is fair to view your initial beliefs as closely approximating those of your caregivers at that time, which has a very high chance of still being their beliefs today, as very few people radically change their core beliefs as adults. Indeed, most people become quite mentally rigid with age.

Two Ways Beliefs Are Transmitted

Limiting beliefs are introduced by your family and community in two primary ways:

1. Beliefs That Are Expressly Taught

From our earliest days, we are immersed in specific frameworks designed to shape our understanding. For example, if you grew up in a traditional Christian household, you would be taught the Christian moral worldview, such as "A is right and B is wrong". This is directly communicated to you.

Customs, traditions, religions—all of these are conveyed mostly through written and oral modalities. Of course, these stretch beyond just your immediate family, so that you also adopt these thoughts and thought patterns through institutions like churches, schools and so on. Again, some of these will be invaluable in your life, and others less so.

2. Beliefs That Are Observed and Modelled

A large portion of the thought patterns that you hold do not come through what you are taught in a direct verbal or written manner, but come through what you observe. You notice the interactions that people have, and how people *react* to others' behaviour as well as to events and circumstances. And so you begin to pick up the thoughts and thought patterns (and the resultant behaviour) of others.

For example, you may have seen how a parent would allow their emotional state to drift to anger or rage when another motorist's behaviour displeased them.

Now, you might think to yourself, "But it did happen: someone did something in traffic which no one would approve of, so isn't that a natural reaction?"

It certainly is the norm *by the standards of society* to react to someone else's behaviour, however, it does not mean that it will be true to your natural state. If you do not know about your Inner Peace and do not care about your proximity to it, then your emotional state is up for the taking. When you see all around you how people *react* to others, then it is easy to accept it as the way that the world works, and how things "have to be".

When you notice the behaviour modelled by others you have two choices: you may adopt that behaviour as your own, or you can identify it as something that you do not want to keep for yourself.

The latter is most likely to be the case if you have more awareness in the moment, and can discern that the lower emotional state accompanying a belief or behaviour does not serve you. This is but one of an infinite number of things that you will observe that can have different influences on your life, depending on how you interact with it. However, just because it is presented to you does not mean that you *have to* adopt it.

Limiting Beliefs: Worth and Conditions

Another common form of a limiting belief is that your worth as a person is dependent on certain achievements or accomplishments of the avatar. This is often accompanied by the need to obtain the approval of others. In this view, value is assigned by society, both to people and their achievements, and therefore people attempt to maximise these things.

Career and Financial Security

When you learn things from society's perspective such as that someone's value as a *person* is dependent on the job they have, their seniority at work, how wealthy they are, how healthy they are, what race they are, what their sexual orientation is, or what their gender is, that is a view from the perspective of the avatar alone. Given that most people identify primarily with the avatar, they usually amplify those beliefs in their behaviour as well as what they communicate directly to you.

For example, you may hear your family talk in a dismissive manner about certain occupations, and you may have taken from this that certain career options are simply off the table. You may have mentioned that you would like to be a musician or an artist and the family was not supportive because they thought that you should be a lawyer like your father, or a doctor like your mother. Now, at the back of your mind, you may have just started to create a thought pattern which says that to be valued you need to have a certain profession.

Often, it comes from a well-meaning place. Your family may support certain careers more because they want you to be financially secure and happy, wishing things to go well for you. But even while well-meaning, their own limiting beliefs can be at the base of their concerns; they do not realise that your happiness is an inside job, and that by syncing up with the Creative Source, you can have abundance in your emotional state *and* in the form of the physical things that you need.

This reminds me of when Jesus said: "Therefore do not worry, saying, 'What shall we eat?' or 'What shall we drink?' or 'What shall we wear?' For the Gentiles strive after all these things, and your heavenly Father knows that you need them. But seek first the kingdom of God and His righteousness, and all these things will be added unto you."

In other words, *seek your Inner Peace first* and allow your actions and decisions to flow from there instead of letting them be determined by worries, concerns, fears and the limiting beliefs of yourself and others, even those from well-meaning family members.

Living Under Expectation

In similar ways, your family, friends or other members of your society may want you to marry someone of a particular class, family, status, or community, because it is in line with their beliefs and expectations. However, the Self has not manifested in this form to live up to the expectations of others, or to behave in a way that makes others feel better about themselves and their situations, or to live a life limited by the beliefs of others.

These are all conditions imposed by the avatar minds of others, and living according to disconnected human minds will keep you in chains.

You are only truly free if you stay true to who you are and live *through* the avatar and not *as* the avatar.

Your Practice
Insights for Application

This chapter explores the limiting beliefs introduced by family and institutions, and how awareness can help you trace the origins of your own thought patterns.

Observed Behaviour is a Decision Point

When you notice behaviour modelled by others, there is a choice: adopt it as your own or recognise it as something that does not serve you. Awareness in the moment is what makes that choice available.

Worth is Not Conditional

The belief that your worth depends on your job, your status, your wealth, or the approval of others is a view from the avatar's perspective alone. Your true worth is not something that can be assigned or taken away by society.

Seek Alignment First

When worries about material security or external approval drive your decisions, the path forward is to seek your Inner Peace first and allow your actions and decisions to flow from there.

Live Through, Not as the Avatar

Living life as the Integrated Self is how you embody peace, joy and love. The expectations of others cannot be a substitute for your Inner Peace.

165

CHAPTER SEVENTEEN
The Path Through Society

IT IS WORTH MENTIONING THAT our discussion so far about the Shackles of Society is not meant to encourage you to fight against society in your mind and in your heart. Resistance is rigid; peace lies in pliability. My intention is simply to shine a light on certain elements that can take you away from your Inner Peace and, therefore, disempower you in the moment.

After all, you did not focus into the avatar form so as *not* to be a part of society and share a space with fellow avatars. Part of the human experience is to interact with others and the world around you, and you knew very well what the world looked like when you decided to experience life through the avatar. But you also did not come here to give up the power to direct your life, and you also did not intend to disallow yourself access to your Inner Peace, or to feel completely disconnected from your *true* nature.

Therefore, even if you are interacting with others who are not in resonance with their Inner Peace, it is helpful to know this: you do not have to adopt their thoughts, thought patterns, or emotional states as your own. In the midst of such interactions, by maintaining awareness, you can discern which thoughts to engage with and which to simply let go.

It may be helpful, while you are out there in the world, to remember that most of the people that you will come into contact with will not have a personal relationship with their Inner Peace, and will therefore not deliberately cultivate their inner (emotional) state. They carry their beliefs with them and some of these will keep them in bondage. That is why you should have compassion when you notice that someone is acting from a lower emotional state; do not judge them or fight against where they are. Rather, treasure your own relationship with Self and shine your light so that others may see it and follow it.

Association with the Avatar: The Root of Resistance

Something that all limiting beliefs have in common is that they change your perspective from one of the Integrated Self, distorting it, to varying degrees, to the perspective of the "disconnected" avatar.

It is rather easy to see why that is the case. All resistance comes from the avatar mind and once your focus has shifted from the avatar, all resistance is dropped. You can change your perspective by changing your focus and therefore your level of integration with Self. Once you have integrated with Self, you can look at life through the eyes of the resistance-free Self. This is what it means to live *through* the avatar, instead of as the avatar.

Focusing Outside the Present Moment

Association with the avatar also brings forth the tendency to focus outside of the present moment, and that in itself can be adopted from society. Because the avatar defines its existence in terms of its past, its labels, and its future, you often find that people give away their power in the moment to exactly these things, and it is this tendency that keeps them bound; for what can other people and external circumstances take away from the Self? Absolutely nothing! But from the avatar they can take everything, and that is at the root of a lot of misery, anxiety, fear and anger, especially when the identity of the avatar is threatened.

Seeking External Approval (The Illusion of Conditional Love)

If you are looking for the approval of others—a common desire passed down from generation to generation—it is the avatar looking to feel valued and loved. The Self never feels the lack of love; it *is* pure love, and therefore an Integrated Self feels whole and loved and does not seek it from others who may or may not be integrated themselves in that moment.

Therefore, again, seek alignment first and then engage with external circumstance (including other people) from that elevated vantage point.

Since many people in the world feel unworthy and unloved, this is frequently portrayed in society (whether demonstrated by the behaviour of others or depicted in media), and therefore easier to include in someone's belief system. For a lot of people this sense of unworthiness comes through in the form of feeling undeserving of abundance, and therefore they do not *allow* themselves to *experience* abundance. If your parents or community taught you that you only get things through self-sacrifice and struggle, then you are likely to keep that thought pattern and it becomes your truth. If you believe that earning money should be an uphill battle, how can that *not* end up being your reality?

Similarly, if you grew up in a house or a community where romantic relationships were unstable, or you were told that love "looks" a certain way, then you may later find that you keep yourself from entering, or staying in, a relationship which is truly worthy of you, and is in harmony with your true state.

There are really infinite possibilities and examples that we can discuss, although once the principles are clear, any situation can be viewed with the same clarity. Let's look at one more example to further demonstrate the concepts.

Let's say you grew up around people who were not integrated with Self, and therefore their behaviour reflected that. They would only show love and appreciation to you if your behaviour was acceptable to them. This sounds pretty standard, right? If you behaved as you should in your mother's eyes, you felt the love and appreciation, and when you didn't behave accordingly, you experienced her anger or irritation.

Before your thoughts get too ahead of you, I'm not saying that a parent doesn't care when they discipline a child. Wielded wisely, discipline can be a very important tool in preparing young minds for navigating the social landscape the avatar will encounter during its lifetime. What I am saying is that from very early on most people start to associate feeling loved and being approved of as something that they need to earn, and that *other people* hold the keys to whether you can feel loved in any moment.

And that, of course, means that later in life you may go to extreme lengths to obtain the approval of others, because you *depend* on their view of you to make you feel loved.

Later in a work setting it can mean that you have difficulty saying no and end up taking on things that you do not actually wish to, but because you really want your colleagues or boss to view you favourably, you may sacrifice yourself to obtain their approval. The thing with people (even those in loving relationships) is that you can do so many things in order to obtain someone's approval, but just one slip-up will reveal a wholly different emotional state from them, if they are not stable in their own alignment.

That's why you cannot let how you feel about yourself be dependent on those around you. A belief that places others' opinions of you above your own alignment will not lead you to the everlasting peace, joy and love that you are seeking. You are then building your emotional house on the sand.

Freeing Yourself: Transforming Limiting Beliefs

If you identify a limiting belief, and you wish to free yourself from it, what do you do?

From our earlier discussion about limiting beliefs, you will recall that a limiting belief is really just a thought pattern with resistance in it; one that may have been energised over years, or decades even, and therefore you cannot stop it by focusing on it with the same perspective. That simply energises it more. You also cannot will it away and think that

that will stop it any more than jumping in front of an oncoming train will stop it.

As the belief has within it resistance, you can approach it in the same way as you would other resistant thoughts, namely you can change your focus whenever the resistance shows up. That can soften the thought in the moment, but if it is a limiting belief that affects a large part of your life, and you encounter it frequently, you may want to look at the section on Transformational Thinking (within Thought Management) and apply that technique to the thought pattern of the limiting belief. That will allow you to de-energise it over time, changing the perspective and the thoughts that you have about it systematically by viewing it as the Integrated Self.

But remember, these thought patterns are highly energised if they are beliefs developed over many years (or decades even!), and therefore it can take some time to shift them.

In the meantime, the more often you approach life as the Integrated Self, the less likely you are to get pulled in by the gravitational pull of those thoughts in the first place, and the more you energise those thoughts that support your alignment.

YOUR PRACTICE
Insights for Application

This chapter considers how we can interact with the world and its varying levels of alignment without adopting the limiting beliefs or emotional states of others.

Be a Conscious Participant

You came to experience life and interact with others, not to fight society. The key is to apply your filter of discernment, so that you do not indiscriminately adopt others' thoughts, thought patterns or emotional states as your own.

Discern and Let Go

Maintaining awareness while in the world allows you to apply your discernment in choosing which thoughts to engage with and which to simply let go.

Practice Compassion, Not Judgement

Many people you encounter are not consciously tending to their minds, their inner states, their actions or reactions. When you notice someone acting from a lower emotional state, approaching them with compassion rather than judgement or conflict serves both of you.

Your Power is Now

Giving away your power by focusing on the past, your labels, or your future in ways that do not serve you is the hallmark of the avatar. The power to direct your life exists solely in the present moment.

Build on the Rock

Basing your emotional state on the approval, behaviours or thoughts of others is building your emotional house on the sand. The stable, consistent foundation of your Self is the rock.

Transforming Limiting Beliefs

A limiting belief is simply a thought pattern with resistance that has been energised over time. It can be approached like any other resistant thought—by redirecting focus when the resistance shows up, or by applying Transformational Thinking to de-energise it systematically.

True Freedom is Internal

Living according to the expectations and limiting beliefs of others is a form of bondage. You are truly free only when you live *through* the avatar and not *as* the avatar.

PART FIVE

Relationships

CHAPTER EIGHTEEN

The Connection Code

RELATIONSHIPS ARE SO INTEGRAL TO the physical experience that it is worth looking at the interplay between your own relationship with your Inner Peace and your relationships with other people—which you'll recall are other focused points of Consciousness, just like you, whether you like, accept and appreciate them or not. Although the discussion up to now truly gives you all of the foundational knowledge to approach life as the Integrated Self in all areas of your life, the nuances of its application in the realm of relationships will be of value to most people.

Your relationships are not things that happen to you; they are co-creations. Every family bond, every friendship and every partnership is constantly being shaped by your energy. We use the Experience Formula as the lens for this section because it perfectly describes this dynamic:

Desire (Pure Intent) − Resistance (Avatar's Fear) = Outcome (The Relationship Reality)

To create relationships rooted in love and joy, the path is always the same: maximise the purity of your desire and minimise the resistance you hold towards the other person and yourself.

The Complexity of Familial Bonds

We will start by looking at the role of relationships in our lives, with a bit more focus on familial relationships, as arguably the most common type of relationship. Just by seeing it mentioned here, you might already be experiencing the activation of certain thoughts or beliefs entering your mind, some more positive than others.

It is through these familial bonds that you probably adopted many of your beliefs and behavioural patterns. That makes these relationships rather complicated at times, as there are so many dimensions to them.

Not only do you typically know these people since birth, but you also step into an established family structure, with well-established beliefs and pre-existing relationships. Some relationships may be very loving and supportive, while others are perhaps weighed down by anger, resentment or envy. It is a complex environment for someone to navigate, especially when they are young and the family essentially makes up their whole world.

Not only are there so many different dynamics *within* a family, but there are also vast differences *between* families, ranging from socio-economic, cultural and religious differences, to differences in power dynamics and how families express their emotions—or don't.

Sometimes, given this wide variety of differences, you may wonder how you were matched up with a particular family. You may think you were just lucky to be blessed with a family that you adore, or you may wonder how you were cursed with the family that you were born into, or anything in-between these extremes.

By now you probably have come to the understanding, either fully or to some degree, that as Consciousness focused into this form, you didn't just randomly *land* somewhere. You came to this experience with certain intentions, including intentions of interactions, and to experience life from a certain perspective. You knew from the perspective of the Self where you would be best placed to satisfy those intentions, and to grow.

To understand these intentions from the perspective of the avatar alone is an impossible task. That is when someone starts to compare their life to those of others, thinking that others had a better deal to start off with. That can easily lead to resentment of the place or family that you come from, or of the body, or of your circumstances growing up. Comparison feeds insecurity.

From the narrow perspective of the avatar alone, you simply cannot see the bigger picture, and then some situations may seem blessed while others seem unfair, or some people seem "lucky" and others are "unlucky". In reality, these things are actually not comparable at all because each experience carries its own weight and emerges from its own singular set of causes.

The common denominator, though, is that all came from Consciousness for the expression and experience of love in all of its forms.

Acceptance: Reclaiming Your Power

That brings me to an important application of the concept I mentioned earlier: you need to accept where you are, and your circumstances, in order to claim your power in the moment.

This is critical if events or circumstances from the past still disempower you frequently enough that they impact your emotional climate.

This could range from remembering elements of your childhood that you do not like, to blaming family members for where you find yourself now. Perhaps you think that you would have had a more successful marriage if your parents had been a better example to you, and did not get divorced when you were 10, or that you would have had a better life if your parents had had more money.

Blaming others (including God, the universe, or anything else) for where you find yourself *now* simply disempowers you and does not help you to shape your *future* moments to be in resonance with your pure desires. When you do this, you are using the *present* moment to direct your energy to thoughts that do not serve you because no matter how much you focus on past circumstances, you cannot change or undo them. Those moments were previous *nows*, and all of your power sits in the current *now*.

A more productive approach is to channel that energy (focus) into strengthening your relationship with your Inner Peace. This will enable you to feel the love and peace that you ultimately want to feel in this moment, and from that emotionally solid ground you can change how you view yourself and your family. You realise that you are the director of your life and you can give control to others or to past events, or you can reclaim your power in the *now*. Accepting the family that you're in, and everything that comes with it, allows you to direct your life, because there is no going back and you want to apply your power to the *now*, over which you *do* have control.

Remember, this isn't about arguing why you are justified in standing in resistance to your family, nor is it saying that everything they did was perfect or wanted, but it is about reclaiming your power from things that do not serve you, which is where acceptance provides the keys to your emotional freedom.

The Role of Family in Your Own Journey

The role that family plays is different for each person, and it is up to you to determine the extent to which you want your family to play a role later in your life. What your initial family or caretakers provide is a platform from which you launch into this life. For the vast majority of people it provides a stable environment while you find your feet in this world, where hopefully your basic needs are looked after. It is also where you learn the foundations of being human and of the world around you. It acts like a seedling tray that allows you to sprout and explore in a reasonably sheltered space until you are in a position to be independent, and depending on your intentions, that platform also made you expand in certain ways that may or may not be evident to you looking back.

Discerning What Serves You

Whatever role your family plays to you, it is worth noting that your family is *not* supposed to be a replacement for the relationship that you have with your Inner Peace, or a substitute for your Inner Guidance.

Just like with the other aspects of the world, there are things in your family structure that are in resonance with your Inner Peace, and things that are not, and therefore you need to discern in all situations and circumstances between the things that serve you and those that do not.

For example, if you have learned from your family to always look for the good in others, that is a wonderful thing which is in resonance with your Inner Peace, so put that mentally in your box of "things that serve me". The contents of this mental box are thoughts and beliefs that support your journey of self-mastery and therefore you wish to interact with more of these in your life.

If your family also believes that your worth is tied to the number of possessions that you have, or how others view you, then that does not support you on your journey of self-mastery and you can place it in the box of "things that do not serve me". This box contains those thought patterns that you do not wish to perpetuate. Instead of fighting against the thought when it shows up, you can simply mentally place it in the box and then shift your attention. It's a visualisation exercise that may help you to let go of a specific thought that you can apply to any topic in your life. Because the thought feels "dealt" with, it may be a helpful trick to help you let go of the thought without interacting with it too much.

Changing or creating family relationships that are in resonance with your Inner Peace is something that most people want for themselves, and we will address that in our next section by looking at how you create and maintain *any* wanted relationship, not just with family.

In summary: we pick up many, if not most, of our most powerful beliefs through our families, and these form part of the societal beliefs that we hold, and it is up to you to decide which ones you wish to perpetuate or release. You don't have to be a slave to unwanted thought patterns and behaviour inherited from your family — *you* get to choose the impact that your family and their beliefs have on your experience here and now.

CHAPTER NINETEEN

Designing Relationships That Thrive

Relationships: The Ultimate Co-Creation

MANY PEOPLE ARE LOOKING FOR someone with whom they can share their life. Some may not have been romantically involved before, or they have been but have not found "the one", or they may have been in wonderful relationships before but due to changing circumstances find themselves looking for a romantic relationship once more. Similarly, people typically seek to create loving relationships with friends and family.

As we have discussed earlier, the Experience Formula applies equally to material and less tangible desires, such as relationships. If you've been looking for a *loving* relationship, but it has not yet materialised, then it is possible that there is some resistance in your thoughts around relationships that is preventing the realisation of what you are looking for in your experience.

Desire vs. Resistance: Where is Your Focus?

Being aware enough to know whether you are energising (amplifying) the "desire" or "resistance" part of the Experience Formula is important. These are so closely related because they are connected to the same topic, and if you do not pay attention, you will not really know whether you are focusing energy *in support of* the desire or *in resistance to* being alone. The distinction is crucial, because the outcomes are very different.

As with all creation, the outcome is determined by what you are doing with your focus in all of the *current* moments. In every moment you are directing energy when you focus. Where you have been focusing in the previous moments determines the reality in the current moment, and how you focus in the current moment will determine what your future moments look like. This is how you create your reality one moment at a time.

Understand that the different aspects of your life overlap, and that your desires and resistances interconnect to an extent. You can have both light and shadow relating to one topic.

For example, if you are looking for a loving relationship, but you feel unworthy, then seeing yourself as unworthy can act as resistance to the realisation of a loving relationship where you are treated with respect, all because you do not feel worthy of your pure desires. That resistance can play out in other areas as well, such as well-being, finances, career and so on. Such resistance makes up part of your emotional climate and therefore can impact the realisation of any and all dreams and desires you may have.

Even so, you do not need to concern yourself with the specific and precise categorisation of your desires and resistances—the same awareness principle applies. When you are thinking about a certain topic and you notice an opposing thought or emotion, you do not have to classify it, judge it or resist it.

A more beneficial approach at that point may be to shift your focus to something else (redirecting your energy), or if it is a recurring thought, then you can look at applying the transformational thinking technique to it. Remember that transformational thinking is done from a stable mental platform, which is why that practice allows you to address such unwanted thoughts *without* being pulled in and further energising those thoughts.

The Power of Inner Peace

In continuing the journey of prioritising your self-mastery and softening resistance thoughts as you go, both direct and indirect resistance on topics will dissolve.

For example, the more time you spend in resonance with your Inner Peace, the more you realise your worthiness as focused Consciousness. This means that thoughts that bring forth feelings of unworthiness, insecurity and so forth, are energised less and less, and therefore start to dissolve—they become less active. In our Experience Formula, this reduces the resistance component, which changes your experience.

From the perspective of the Integrated Self, you will also get a better view of your pure desires, which further energises the thoughts of them. Thus by practising aligning with your eternal perspective, your emotional climate shifts, and you generally focus more on those thoughts that are in resonance with your Inner Peace, as opposed to resistant thoughts.

Avoiding the "How" Trap

In practising self-mastery, which is really the mastery of the mind, you may wonder how that *practically* brings you closer to realising the relationship (romantic or otherwise) that you are looking for. This is where you want to avoid the trap of obsessing over the details of how it can happen, which brings doubt and attachment to an outcome into the equation. You simply want to reach a point where you *allow* it to happen, without it being a condition for you to enter your Inner Peace. By allowing it, you allow the myriad of ways in which something can be realised to be revealed to you.

That does not mean that you do not take any action, but it does mean that you take action as the Integrated Self, while following your Inner Guidance. The Self views your situation from a higher perspective and can therefore guide you to where you truly want to be. And when you approach life as the Integrated Self, you are in a position to receive that guidance.

Such guidance comes through as a pull, a knowing, an inspiration, or can come through interactions with others, among other ways. But you have to be in a place of awareness and allowance to see it for what it is. It does not come with a big neon sign saying "This Way", and you still have a choice whether you want to follow the guidance or not, just like you can obey the GPS or not when you are driving around in a strange city. Practically speaking, it is easy to imagine the difference between the relationships that you create from a place of desperation and a fear of being alone, and those relationships that form because you're in love with yourself and joyously experiencing life.

Discerning Empowering Thoughts

Similar to the process of allowing the guidance to flow to you, it is also of great value to know when to daydream about your pure desire, and when it is best not to focus on it. If you are prone to obsessive thinking, then it is especially helpful to remove focus sooner rather than later if the thoughts do not serve you, which is when they do not direct the energy in support of your pure desire. To know whether you are channelling energy in support of your pure desires or not, you need to be able to discern between supportive and non-supportive thoughts, which we can also call empowering and disempowering thoughts.

Measuring Thoughts Against Inner Peace

You measure your thoughts by their compatibility with your Inner Peace. As your thoughts will have an emotional state equivalence that you can pick up on, you can assess them against the emotional state of your Inner Peace and see whether they are compatible. You can also try evaluating it the other way around: first get into a solid place in your Inner Peace, and then see whether you still have access to that thought by revisiting the subject. From this perspective you can see the clear distinction between empowering and disempowering thoughts. Here you will often think quite differently about something or someone because you are looking at it or them from the perspective of the Integrated Self, where the mind is in resonance with the perspective of the Self, and therefore also of Consciousness. Note, when I refer to these as separate, it is merely a demarcation of what is in essence all "One", ultimately.

When we speak here about empowering and disempowering thoughts, we include both thoughts that are *specific* to that particular topic, as well as your *general* thoughts. *All* of your thoughts and beliefs impact how you direct your focus, your energy, and therefore impact whether you have embraced your inner Creative Power.

Pockets of Resistance

Another thing to be mindful of are those pockets of resistance we discussed earlier. You could be *generally* aligned with the perspective of the Self in most areas of your life but still hold resistance in a few specific areas. However, such pockets of resistance can still have an impact on how you experience certain aspects of your life.

For example, you could allow abundance into your life in areas of money, career, family relationships and so forth, while you at the same time have beliefs specific to romantic relationships which hold you back from realising the romantic relationship that you are looking for. In other words, your emotional climate does play a role in letting things into your experience or not, seeing as it influences your general level of resistance, but that does not necessarily translate into the negation of the resistance on a specific topic, especially if it is highly energised. It does make it easier to soften the resistance on a topic if you generally are able to come into alignment fairly quickly and have many other topics that you can look at to help to stabilise your alignment. In short, a generally positive emotional climate will make many things easier for you, but you may still have to resolve pockets of resistance on specific topics in order to be in alignment with your Self's perspective on the topic. For that, you can address the pockets individually, and apply the transformational thinking technique to help clear them up.

Why Your Focus Matters

It is important to keep your focus on what you are looking to create during this process. It is extremely tempting to let *what is* get more of your attention than *what is unfolding*. And that is why, for most people, their lives don't really change that much: they base their thought interactions on what they are observing, and channel their energy into *what is,* which therefore creates more of the same for the future moments.

We are continuous creators, and it's this ability to mould energy to create your reality that sits at your core and can be used to either create more of what you really want, or what you do not want.

For example, let's say that you are in the process of bringing the right romantic partner for you into your life. By focusing on the absence of a romantic partner, such as by lamenting over how you currently don't have someone, nurturing envy over your friends and their romances, feeling sorry for yourself on Valentine's Day, or repeatedly wondering when and how that special person will enter your life—you are repeatedly telling yourself that you are lonely. That, of course, only serves to energise the state which is *in opposition* to what you *truly* want. Your creation is going to be centred around "I am lonely", and that creates your experience, albeit without intending to: a life filled with loneliness.

Similarly, suppose you have come out of a relationship that ended because the person was working too much and did not have enough time to spend with you. If you keep active in your mind that you are looking for "someone who isn't married to their job" or "someone who isn't as selfish as person X", then you are actually emphasising the parts of the relationship that you did *not* want. It doesn't matter how you're phrasing it. The fact remains that your entire quest's emphasis is on the lack that you felt in your previous relationship. It is all about whether the thought itself is in resonance with your Inner Peace (and remember that the Consciousness that dwells in you does not create out of any sort of lack). That way you can phrase things exactly the same, yet in the one way you could be directing energy in the direction of your pure desire, while in the other you could be directing the energy in opposition to that desire. It all comes down to being aware enough of whether the thought itself is empowering or not.

How would a better version of the above thoughts look? How about "I'm going to open myself to finding someone to love me and meet all my romantic needs, just like I am going to meet their romantic needs." A small change verbally, sure, but doesn't that already *feel* much more empowering? Doesn't it *feel* more allowing?

Creating Versus Escaping

There is also a distinction between focusing on the relationship that you are wanting to create and using thoughts of the future to escape *what is*. Similar to being aware of your other thoughts, you can use your awareness to distinguish between dreaming and escaping. Dreaming can be an act of directed creation, while escaping is much less powerful, based as it is on avoidance, which resonates at a much lower emotional range.

When you are thinking about your ideal partner, their wonderful qualities and your future moments, you are directing pure energy to the green bucket of pure desire. But when you use thoughts of a future relationship as a means to escape a current feeling of loneliness, you are merely feeding the red bucket of resistance.

The Experience Formula shows the power difference (using arbitrary numbers for purposes of illustration):

Desire – Resistance = Outcome

Dreaming (Low Resistance):
10 – 2 = +8 (Intended Outcome)

Escaping (High Resistance):
10 – 15 = –5 (Unintended Outcome, fuelled by lack)

In the case where you are doing it in order to escape your current situation, your thoughts are more centred around the idea of "I wish I had that, because I feel incomplete or empty without it," which channels your focus and your energy more in the direction of desperately trying to change your situation than towards your pure desire and what you are looking to create. When feelings of loneliness or lack are dominant, you are outside of your Inner Peace, and you are no longer empowered to direct your experience.

That is why it is so beneficial to be in close proximity to your Inner Peace, because then not only do you already feel whole, loved and worthy, but in this state you will also create from a place of being empowered.

In our two scenarios here, because you *feel* at peace when you are in alignment, you do not create from a place of *needing* to change what is. You rather get into a place of allowing, and in that state you are better attuned to the things that you want to experience, and can therefore more readily "dream" about those things. Also, from that place, you are empowered and channelling energy in the direction that is supportive of the realisation of your pure desires.

It really is all about getting yourself in a state of allowance to open yourself up to those things that you want to include in your experience, while understanding that what you are ultimately reaching for is your Inner Peace, and it is from that place that a relationship may sprout.

YOUR PRACTICE
Insights for Application

This chapter highlights that relationships are co-creations and that the most effective way to shape them is by mastering your internal focus and aligning with your Inner Peace.

The Relationship Experience Formula

The reality of your relationships is constantly shaped by your energy:

Desire (Pure Intent) – Resistance (The Avatar's Fear) = Outcome (The Relationship Reality)

Prioritise Inner Peace

Seeking a relationship to substitute or provide your Inner Peace creates from a place of lack rather than wholeness. Being whole, loved and worthy first ensures the relationship is an add-on, not a crutch.

Discern Desire vs. Lack

When focusing on finding a partner, being aware of your underlying emotion matters. Thoughts centred on loneliness ("I wish I had that, because I feel incomplete") add resistance (feeding the red bucket). Thoughts centred on the joyful qualities you wish to share are pure desire (feeding the green bucket).

Avoid the "How" Trap

Obsessing over the specific mechanics of how a relationship will materialise introduces doubt and attachment. Reaching a state of allowance lets the myriad of possibilities be revealed to you by Inner Guidance.

Watch Your Words and Focus

Focusing on what you don't want (e.g., "someone who isn't selfish") amplifies resistance, even when the intention behind it *seems* positive. Energising the positive qualities and attributes you wish to experience directs your creative energy towards your pure desire.

Use Awareness in Daydreaming

There is a distinction between true, directed creation (dreaming) and using future thoughts to escape your present situation (escaping). Escaping is avoidance rooted in resistance and will not lead to a fulfilling outcome.

CHAPTER TWENTY

Nurturing Relationships That Thrive

IN THE PREVIOUS CHAPTER WE looked at how to create relationships from a place of alignment. But what about the relationships already in your experience?

Keeping the Right Relationship

You may already have a wonderful relationship and might be wondering how to keep it, especially if you see so many people around you separating after being together for many years, or when relationships with family members go off the rails. There are several factors that come together to drive how a relationship changes over time, so let's unpack some of these together.

When most people get into a new relationship, they tend to have good expectations of what is to come and look at the other person with a focus on their positive and attractive attributes. This is the famous "honeymoon period", during which the world and life may just seem better to you.

As with anything else, once the newness has worn off, it no longer draws your attention as much and in the same way. If your emotional state is determined by the people and things around you, you may find yourself in a similar emotional state to the one you were in before you went into this relationship. To that extent the relationship may have distracted you temporarily from other unwanted things that may normally grab your focus and in that way pull you out of alignment. When the new relationship started up, your focus shifted to things more positive and you probably spent more time being present in the moment, which helped you to maintain better emotional weather.

Once the newness wears off, your focus may return to those things which were on your mind before. In other words, you may have experienced a change in your emotional weather, but now your perception is returning to the typical range of your emotional climate.

At this point your attention may shift from focusing on the positive attributes of your partner to dwell more on the aspects that you do not like, and the same applies to the relationship overall. As you focus more on those things, you channel your energy in that direction, which only amplifies and energises it more, which, as we already know, will have implications for your future moments.

If you have been paying attention, you will already be able to guess that focusing on the unwanted aspects of a relationship will create, over time, an unwanted outcome.

That works twofold: firstly, by introducing resistance, you get in the way of allowing the desired relationship to remain in your experience. In our Experience Formula, you are increasing the amount of resistance, which decreases the value (positivity) of the outcome. Secondly, by consistently channelling energy to (by putting your focus on) the unwanted attributes of your partner and your relationship, you energise the state at which those thoughts exist and bring more of the things that match that state into your experience. This will most often manifest as problems in the relationship itself, but it can also come through in other aspects of your life. That is because sufficiently energising a particular emotional state can bring down your general emotional climate. It is the amount of energy you put into any emotional state that determines to what extent things of that nature are included in your experience.

The Trolley Dash

When I was younger there used to be a show on television: a toy store trolley dash, where a kid would have three minutes to load as many toys or games as he could into his trolley, and then get to take those toys home for free.

Life works a little like that trolley dash. You are that lucky kid who is put in this world, and you get to choose what you want to include in your experience. The way that you include things in your trolley is to give your focus (and therefore your energy) to them.

Your *focusing* is how you *choose*.

With this image in mind, consider asking yourself why you are focusing on certain unwanted, negative things, if that focus is precisely what keeps that thing in your experience, and is possibly even expanding it. It most certainly takes some practice not to let the conditions and the people around you determine how you apply your focus, and therefore determine how you feel in the present moment. Ultimately, to have the experiences that you want, you need to be disciplined in directing your focus.

Practically speaking, in a relationship, that would mean that you do not let the attributes or parts of your partner or family member that typically bother you be the things that you judge and primarily focus on when you think about the person or the relationship.

You should remain aware enough to notice when unwanted thoughts enter your mind, and also pay attention to your emotional state, as your thoughts have an impact on your proximity to your Inner Peace. By doing so, you will be able to tell when your emotional state has changed. You can also tell which thoughts are most active in you on the subject of the person or the relationship by seeing what types of thoughts come up when you think about them. If these are mostly non-aligned thoughts, then you know that resistance-inducing thoughts are currently the most active around the subject.

Influence Over Others

When we talk about changing your perspective on your partner or your relationship, it is from a place of understanding that you can *influence* how people and situations interact with you, and that the world acts as a mirror to you. That is absolutely true.

Remember, our focus here is on self-mastery and making adjustments to the part of the relationship over which you have control, which are your energetic and physical contributions to the relationship. However, that does not mean that there isn't communication between you and your partner about things that you want to change in the relationship. But you can have a much more productive conversation if you first realign your mind as much as possible before you engage in any conversations with your partner relating to the relationship and to maintain awareness of your mind and inner state throughout the conversation. You then set yourself up for a much more empowered conversation because now you're bringing your Self into it. Such a conversation can even help you to clear up some of your own resistant thoughts about yourself, your partner or the relationship.

When Resistance is Dominant

However, when a situation is so resistance-laden that it poses a risk to your safety, then it is best that you first remove yourself from the situation. Any relationship is truly a co-creation, and as you do not have complete control over someone else's behaviour and creations (because they are a co-creator too), you need to be honest with yourself about what *is* under your control when you make decisions.

In a highly stressed environment it is much more difficult to enter your Inner Peace and to remain empowered. When something unwanted is in your field of awareness and is highly energised, it can feel like you simply cannot change how you think about it, which leaves you powerless. If you think of the Experience Formula, if the level of resistance in a situation is really high, then the outcome (experience) will be really negative too, and leaving the situation may be the best option for now, so you can regain control of your experience.

That being said, once you have withdrawn from such a situation, it is really important to clean up some of your resistance on the subject, otherwise you may end up in a very similar situation the next time around, or you might even find yourself going back to the situation from which you had to escape. This is often how people go from one relationship to another, but they seem to have a *type* of person or relationship that they always return to.

In other words, take care to change your inner world with regard to the subject so that your outer world on the subject can also change. Often when people enter unwanted relationships, it is from a place of insecurity, loneliness, or not feeling worthy. That is not the type of platform from which you can launch a successful and fulfilling relationship.

On the other hand, things that are "small annoyances" in the relationship and which you continue to focus on and fight against, and do not clear up or let go of, become further energised. Remember, though, that clearing up resistant thoughts or letting go of resistant thoughts is not the same as suppressing recurring unwanted thoughts! When you engage with a thought (in any manner) on a recurring basis but do not acknowledge it, or when you judge the thought for existing in the first place, you do not truly let go of it. Biting your tongue and bearing something is not the same as accepting the existence of the thought but choosing to not engage with it any further.

With sufficient energy poured into the unwanted aspects of the relationship, your inner world becomes active with the state of annoyance, and continues to move to lower emotional states as you continue to energise the movement in that direction. In that way you may end up with a relationship that is wholly unwanted, and it starts on a slippery slope of not being aware in most moments of how you are applying your energy, and not taking care to change course if you notice your mind heading off in an unwanted direction.

Where Relationships and Emotional Climates Intersect

In certain instances, it can be that you and your partner were in different emotional climates when you started the relationship compared to the states you are in now. Since you are in a different place, it makes sense that your relationship will also have to evolve to remain relevant to your experience.

So let's say that you have a more positive emotional climate than you used to have when you started the relationship. As your life will start to reflect your new inner state, your relationship will also have to change to remain relevant to this new state. For most relationships, this would mean a wonderful change because you can connect with someone on a deeper level than you ever have before, simply because more of your true nature is becoming part of this relationship. At other times, it may mean that there is a better relationship out there for you, which is also change but in a different way.

If you are in a relationship that resonates with your true nature, and you wish to keep this wonderful relationship, then continuing to channel energy into it in a way that does not introduce resistance to it and to your view of your partner, is the way in which you sustain and grow this relationship; you are essentially keeping it as a *wanted* relationship in your experience.

How you think about it and how you talk about it all forms part of the energy that you channel to it and which elements of the relationship you choose to energise. It comes down to the little things that build up into how you channel energy to the relationship overall. Do you appreciate your partner in your interactions with them? Do you see them for who they truly are and focus on the parts of them that form part of their true nature? Do you look at yourself, your partner and your relationship from the perspective of the Integrated Self, or do you view it from the perspective of the avatar alone?

In other words, be aware of your mind and your thoughts, and guard them so that you can direct your life and have a relationship with your Inner Peace. By seeking your Inner Peace first before you look to create something or interact with others, you put yourself in a position where you can create relationships that simply are not possible from the avatar's perspective and ability alone.

Disagreements and Conflict

As we all know, human interaction is a complex subject, and because there are as many worlds as there are perspectives, there will be times when realities, expectations, perspectives or beliefs will overlap with others, and times when they won't. But even in those circumstances, you can have a different view to someone else on something while still being in alignment during the interaction, even if *they* are not, or do not remain, in alignment.

The Turning Point in Conflict

Should you hold a different view to someone else, but you start sacrificing your alignment to get your point across, then you start to disempower yourself. It is for that turning point that you should keep a lookout, as it is easier to turn it around when it hasn't gone very far.

The best question to ask yourself in this circumstance is *why* you would sacrifice your alignment for a disagreement. For a lot of arguments, people feel that they really need to defend their view. And while the act of expressing your view in itself does not change your proximity to your Inner Peace, if you introduce thoughts that include judgement and blame, then it will start to take you away from your Inner Peace. This can go right down to anger or beyond if the people arguing are energising those lower emotional states through the argument. If you notice that this tends to happen to you, then you may want to get a better understanding of *why* you attach to their behaviour or the interaction in a way that comes at the cost of your own alignment with your Self.

The Need to be Right

For a lot of people it comes down to a feeling of needing to be right. We are not talking about believing in your own viewpoint and sharing that view, but something that comes from a place of needing others to agree with you or validate your view. That "need" arises from identifying so much with the view that it forms part of the identity of the avatar—and the avatar can easily feel attacked if its so-called "identity" is challenged! That's why the avatar often wants its identity to be recognised (i.e. validated) by others.

Looking at it another way, someone can measure their worth by what they know, or their views and beliefs, and if someone else does not agree with that, it challenges the person on their value metric and can be interpreted as a threat. The fact is that most people in the world care more about being right than they do about mastering their mind.

There is a whole spectrum of emotions that can come up during an interaction with someone, but it is important to stay aware enough to identify when your thoughts have a negative emotional pull to them. It often starts with annoyance or frustration during the interaction—these are the initial signals that the thoughts have moved to point in opposition to your Inner Peace. At this point, it may be helpful to first disengage from the conversation or even to let your partner know that your emotional state is wavering to help them understand where you are. If they are stable in their alignment, they can even hold a space for you to help you return to your true nature.

Conflict: A Self-Mastery Opportunity

Of course, there can be arguments or disagreements in a relationship about many topics, taking many forms. Differences in opinion surface fairly regularly for most people, whether in work situations, in a family setting, or with your romantic partner. It may be about something serious or less serious.

Arguments may not be about a difference of opinion at all. They can be about an agreement that was broken, or something that someone has said or done. The exact conditions are endless, but in the end, the principles remain the same. When you are interacting with someone, you ultimately still have control over your mind and focus, and therefore over your level of empowerment, and it is here where true mastery of the mind comes in. You have a choice to view situations either from the perspective of the avatar alone, or, by learning to direct your thoughts and focus, from the perspective of the Integrated Self.

Letting Go of the Past

Because people have so many relationships across the lifespan of the avatar, and some of these go back to the time that you were born, for many people a lot of the discord that they feel in the present moment is a result of experiences from the past that they relive in the present. These can be experiences from a previous marriage or relationship, or from being bullied at school, or from how they were treated in their childhood home. For many, that pain becomes a part of their identities, because the avatar identifies itself largely in terms of its experiences.

There are many things that people do to each other that no one with love in their heart would want another to experience, but the fact remains that when people are acting as the avatar alone, they often treat others in a way that is in complete opposition to their true natures.

However, the avatar's past actually does not define who you *truly* are at all. The identity of that eternal part of you is not defined by its experiences — you *simply are* in this moment, and the next, and the next.

And your power is not in the past. You can only decide whether to give your power away *to* the past, or to empower yourself in this now.

It's never worth letting previous misaligned behaviour from you or someone else determine your level of alignment *now*. Jesus spoke to this when he said to forgive those you have grievances with: "…not up to seven times, but up to seventy times seven." The reason is that you simply cannot be in alignment with your true nature and be empowered in this moment if you are fighting against something from the past or against another's behaviour. Your eternal perspective simply does not hold onto anger, judgement, resentment and so forth, the same way as human minds do, and that puts you in dissonance with your true nature.

The Buddha echoed this sentiment when he said, "'He abused me, he laughed at me, he struck me.' Thus one thinks and so long as one retains such thoughts one's anger continues."

Does Self-Mastery Mean I Cannot Stand Up for What Is Right?

That is not the message at all. The message is about self-love, self-mastery, empowerment and taking back the control to steer your life. That is what's at the heart of focusing into this form of the avatar: you are a Creator at your core, and you did not set forth to come here and then just give away your Creative Power.

When people look through the eyes of the avatar alone, they see fighting as strength, not realising that you sacrifice your own power in the very moment that you fight against something. Looking through the eyes of the Integrated Self, you could notice a condition that can be improved, or you can see that someone is misaligned, but you assist through remaining in your true power and effecting change in a way the avatar alone cannot achieve.

Being a Light to the world is not only the way to use your own Creative Power for the betterment of your experience and that of others, but it is also the way that others can step into their own true power too: by you being a Light for them to reveal their own Light, which was in them all along, but obscured.

It's not about being blind or not having a conviction, but it *is* about directing your focus to remain in your Inner Peace, and understanding how you can draw on the assistance of the Self to effect change, and caring enough about being empowered that you focus in a way that supports that alignment *irrespective* of how others may view it.

Most of the world looks to physical action and reaction as signs of strength, but you shouldn't put your alignment on the line to look to the world on what mastery of self and strength look like. Measure your strength and mastery by how empowered you are, as that is what allows you to actually direct your life.

Let your measure be the amount of peace, joy and love that you allow yourself to experience in any given moment.

YOUR PRACTICE
Insights for Application

This chapter addresses how to sustain, navigate and grow the relationships already in your experience, using the same principles of focus and alignment.

Your Focusing is How You Choose

In a relationship, what you give your focus to is what you energise. Dwelling on the unwanted attributes of your partner or relationship channels energy in that direction. Choosing to focus on what you appreciate sustains and grows the relationship you want to keep.

Relationships Evolve with Your Emotional Climate

As your emotional climate shifts, your relationships will either evolve to match your new state or lose their relevance to your experience. Continuing to channel energy into a relationship without introducing resistance is how you nurture it.

Know When to Step Away

When a situation is so resistance-laden that it poses a risk to your safety, removing yourself is the most empowered choice. Self-mastery means being honest about what is under your control and being kind to yourself.

The Need to Be Right

The need for others to validate your view arises from the avatar identifying so strongly with its beliefs that any challenge feels like a threat. Caring more about your alignment than about being right is to walk the path of self-mastery.

Your Power is Not in the Past

Reliving past relationship pain in the present keeps those thought patterns active and energised. Your power sits in the current now. Letting go is about reclaiming your power from what no longer serves you.

CHAPTER TWENTY-ONE

Holding the Light in Relationships

YOU HAVE FOCUSED INTO THIS avatar form, into this time, into this world, knowing very well that a large part of your experience here would involve interacting with others—focused Consciousness playing together in these physical containers we call the avatars.

These relationships and interactions are invaluable to everyone's (and Consciousness') growth and expansion and are quite often the catalysts for people to search for their Inner Peace and Guidance. And yes, because of the big role that relationships play in your life, most people experience relationships as a source of joy and love, as well as a source of frustration or anger. There is certainly a lot of variety in what you can experience through relationships in this world! But all of these have contributed to your expansion and experiences here and therefore have value from that perspective.

Because of their importance, we will consider some of the forms of interaction and influence that impact our relationships in further detail together.

Interactions with People Out of Alignment

Given the large number of people in the world, you will interact with people with varying proximities to their Inner Peace. Just because someone has not specifically pursued a journey of self-mastery does not mean that they cannot be in alignment with their true nature. Everyone's Inner Peace already exists, it is merely a matter of focusing into it (or not), and it does not have to be deliberate, of course. Practising self-mastery simply means being actively aware of your proximity to your Inner Peace and adjusting your focus to *deliberately* return to alignment if you have focused in a manner that takes you away from your Inner Peace.

The Mirror Effect

Relationships as Reflections

By this time, you will be quite familiar with the understanding that someone has an emotional state range, which in the short term we refer to as their emotional weather, and over the longer term as their emotional climate.

From that understanding it is rather easy to see how one person's emotional climate may or may not overlap with someone else's. Also, because it really is an average *range*, you can "connect" with quite a diverse selection of people, because it is the overlapping of the ranges that can match you up with other people. How well you match with others is dependent on the extent to which you are in range of each other.

Keep in mind that *matching up* does not necessarily mean getting along with or not. Even when you are a match to someone else, that does not mean that you have to be friends, or even like each other; their *state* overlaps with yours and therefore you are within "range of reception" of each other.

For example, two people can meet each other on the plane of despair or anger and act as mirrors of that state to each other, as well as energisers of that emotional state for each other.

How well you match up with someone can also be seen as how much focus, attention and thus energy the other person draws from you, i.e. the extent to which someone is included in or influencing your experience. Again, your life experience acts as a mirror to your emotional state.

Similarly, other topics such as events that cross your path also have states and ranges at which they exist and come into play in people's lives. How well you match up with a particular event can again be seen as *how much* focus and *what kind* of focus the event gets from you, which determines the extent to which it can affect your experience. If it is something that does not find any resonance with your perspective and established thought patterns, then its impact on your experience will be quite limited.

If you are stable in your Inner Peace, you may notice an outside world event, but you will not give your focus or your energy to it. It will be like the wind that simply blows through your hair.

This principle is reflected in Jesus's parable of the wise builder: "The rain fell, the torrents raged, and the winds blew and beat against that house; yet it did not fall, because its foundation was on the rock."

In other words, there may be external events happening around you, and while you would not deny their existence, you simply do not have to allow them to influence your proximity to your Inner Peace. For example, by learning *not* to judge the actions of others, you can reach a point where someone may insult you, yet it does not impact your emotional state. Instead of being offended, you look at them through your eternal eyes. You may then think to yourself: "How can I help this person return to their natural state?"

But there's more to it than just dealing with things in an aligned state when they cross your path—which is, of course, ideally how you want to face things.

Reaction Reveals Resistance

If a thought pattern is very active in you, you will normally have a *strong* attachment to what is shown to you.

What is your reaction to what you observe? If someone is outside of their Inner Peace and shows you behaviour of that nature, what is active in you determines to what extent that person is relevant to, and therefore "in" your experience.

Let me explain this with a simple example. If Person A says something that can trigger Person B to feel unworthy, but Person B is solid in their knowledge of their true nature, which is one of worthiness and love, then what Person A says is really irrelevant to Person B's experience. You may have empathy for where the person is, but from there you simply move on. On the other hand, if it is a sore spot, you may have a moderate or severe reaction, and that person has just become very prominent in your experience. That interaction may define your whole day, and you may relive the interactions countless times thereafter. In that way, someone acted as a mirror to a pocket of resistance within you. Our reaction reveals the extent to which another person's behaviour resonates with our own inner state.

To help determine what someone's role is in your life that had an impact for better or for worse, you can also revisit what has been on your mind lately: does it seem like what you are observing could be something that you know you've been giving your attention to? Or have you perhaps been unaware of how much time you've been giving to a subject or things of a particular emotional state, so that this may be a useful indicator to you of what you have been focusing on? Have you been taking care to direct your mind and your positive interactions are evidence of that discipline you've been applying?

The Role of Conscious Intention

At other times someone may be relevant to your experience not as an indicator of your emotional climate, but as a result of other things that you may be asking for (and therefore think about) in your experience.

For example, if you like to assist people in financial need, then people experiencing lack in terms of money will become relevant to your experience. This is not because you are feeling deficient, but because you are seeking interactions with people who have a particular need. Think about a doctor who keeps seeing sick people all day. Do you think that's because he or she is channelling sickness and infirmity and therefore creating that reality around them? Of course not. Sick people enter a doctor's experience specifically because he or she wishes to assist those who want to get better.

Sometimes, based purely on the setup of your life or your passions or your skill set, you will be asking to interact with specific people, and those who are a match to that will become relevant to your experience.

Emotional Climate: The Long-Term Shift

Remember that all people have an average emotional state which they cultivate—their emotional climate. That means that in order to understand someone's relevance to your experience, you may have to look beyond your current emotional state—your emotional weather. Because going into your Inner Peace in this moment does not mean that everything physical in your experience which isn't compatible with that is suddenly removed from your experience all at once. Our thoughts and beliefs (as well as the things they bring into our experience) have *momentum* and *inertia*. The states which you energise over time play an important role in the things that are relevant to your experience. As such, you can shift your emotional climate *over time*, and your world responds to that change. That means that your experience, your reality, will shift over time in response to changes in your emotional climate.

The Power of Emotional Dominance in the Moment

With sufficient flow of energy in the moment while you are in alignment, and with the absence of resistance, you can make leaps in terms of the changes that you can effect in your environment, both physically and in terms of the people that you interact with.

You can influence your interactions with other people, and to that extent your own proximity to your Inner Peace plays an active role in the moment. Even if someone has entered your experience now based on a pocket of resistance that you still have, in this moment you get to choose how you interact with the person here and now, irrespective of how the person has entered or remained in your experience so far. Your power is in the now, in this moment, and your influence and interaction is determined by this moment. It is also in this moment that you set up your interaction for future moments, and therefore you can move a series of interactions with someone in a specific direction.

Remember that you radiate your emotional state, your proximity to your Inner Peace, to those around you, and they pick up on that, consciously or subconsciously. It is partly through this interaction of the emotional states that people can influence one another. For example, aren't you a lot more likely to improve someone else's emotional state if you are friendly and kind and share a sincere smile with them?

Ultimately, the person who is planted more firmly in their emotional state dominates the interaction, and therefore your interaction with someone who is far from their Inner Peace can present you with an opportunity to draw that person into alignment, but only if you stand firmly in *your* Inner Peace. If the other person is too firmly entrenched in their lower emotional state, and they are not moving into alignment, at least you can maintain yours, and the interaction will then not have much impact on your experience.

If this mismatch remains, the two of you will soon become irrelevant to each other's experience.

It is interesting to note that sometimes, if you are steady in your alignment, someone who is out of alignment can see that interaction as something that further energises their lower emotional state, even though their own thoughts are energising that state. It is part of how the world is a mirror to *them*.

For example, if the person that you are interacting with feels insecure and sorry for themselves, then when you don't join them in that emotional state they might see that as a further rejection, and end up feeling *more* sorry for themselves due to the lens through which they are viewing the world. All they can see is victimhood and rejection.

These situations can be a challenge, and in order to avoid being pulled under with such a person, you just want to let your focus remain in resonance with your Inner Peace. It is never worth sacrificing your own alignment and moving towards their emotional state (perhaps in a naive attempt to "meet them half-way"), as it is only by remaining steadfast in your own alignment that you are in the best, most empowered position to be truly of assistance to them. After all, a light cannot overcome darkness by dimming itself.

Responding to Those Out of Alignment

That brings us to another point in our discussion, namely how to view and respond to people out of alignment.

As we've discussed earlier, remember that people operate in a typical emotional range, their emotional climate. Within this range, and occasionally outside of it, people will be in different in-the-moment emotional states (their emotional weather). Because of this continuous variance, you will notice people being in alignment and out of alignment at different times. When someone is out of alignment, the type of interaction you will see from them very often leads people to react to that behaviour, even if it means they sacrifice their own alignment in the process, simply because the misaligned behaviour feels personal.

For example, if someone is mean to you or angry with you, it is harder not to give your attention to that, and shifting your attention to it means your focus tends to no longer be in resonance with your Inner Peace because of what you think about what you're focusing on. Of course, ultimately it all depends on how stable you are in your own alignment, and how much resistance is active in your emotional weather and emotional climate—these factors will determine whether you are able to observe someone's behaviour and avoid attaching to it. When you feel good, you tend to have a lot more patience and can shrug things off, while things bother and annoy you a lot more when you are feeling down.

That means that your emotional state determines whether you should remain in the presence of someone who is showing out-of-alignment behaviour—that is, if you truly value your own alignment. If you know that you still react to certain things, it may be easier to avoid it altogether, or to remove yourself from that behaviour whenever it enters your awareness. When you *do* find that behaviour in your experience in the moment, and you *do* find yourself attaching to it, it can be valuable information to clue you in on what may be active within you that causes you to attach to that behaviour. You can get a feel for the pockets of resistance remaining within you merely by observing how certain behaviours trigger you.

The View from the Integrated Self

When you look at the person from the perspective of the Integrated Self, you won't just see the behaviour of the disconnected avatar, but see the person for who they truly are: focused Consciousness, just like you. Even though the avatar may have focused itself into an emotional state which is outside of its own Inner Peace, the core essence will always remain. The true you exists beyond fleeting thoughts and emotional states. It is your rock.

Reacting to that "bad" behaviour as the avatar simply lets out-of-alignment actions grow and expand, both for the person who originally showed it and the person who focused on and attached to it.

Remember: you cannot fight darkness with more darkness.

Rather, only by shining your light to all—those in the light *and* those in the darkness—can you have the opportunity to bring others into the light.

That puts a completely different spin on it. Now seeing someone act out of a place of misalignment is not something to fear or to fight against. Now it is an opportunity to clear your own resistance, to become more stable in your own alignment, and to spread the light to others.

Practical Steps: How to Stop Attaching (Reacting)

In the end it all comes down to the thoughts that are generally active in you and your ability to focus with precision. We can look at two ways to help yourself not react (attach) to what you observe as easily.

Decrease Resistance Systematically

The first is working to systematically decrease and soften your resistant thoughts over time. It is exactly those resistant thought patterns that cause someone to attach to others' behaviour. This shifts your emotional climate to a higher level overall, and therefore, through life acting as a mirror, you will have less of the lower emotional state behaviour active in your experience.

As we've discussed earlier, there may also be other reasons why someone is relevant to your experience, so if someone shows out-of-alignment behaviour, and you do not have active resistance on the subject, usually it will be quite a bit easier to simply observe the behaviour and not attach to it than if it was a match to an energised thought pattern in you. Generally speaking, if you are not triggered by the behaviour, then most likely it's not rooted in any sort of active resistance within you.

Solidify Your Inner Peace

The second way to help yourself not attach to out-of-alignment behaviour is to place yourself firmly focused on your Inner Peace before you interact with others. Even if you have resistance on a subject, being firmly aligned energises those higher range emotional states and therefore makes it harder for your thoughts to be pulled in another direction. Having even more awareness of your thoughts and emotional state while you are interacting with someone showing misaligned behaviour will assist you in identifying when you might start moving away from your Inner Peace. That allows you to adjust your focus in those early moments when the gravitational pull of the thoughts around the behaviour you see is not that strong yet and it is easier to change the direction of your thoughts.

Sensitivity as a Tool

Awareness implies a necessary sensitivity to your thoughts. Because we can so easily get used to our frequent thoughts, it becomes harder to assess whether they are beneficial to us or not. Like with cold, your sense of your own thoughts and emotional state can also be numbed over time. You may have been in a particular state for so long that it's hard to feel or identify it. Sometimes it is only when life holds up a mirror that you realise where your focus has been.

That's why it is good to cultivate a sensitivity to changes in your emotional state, as it allows you to tell when you are heading in a direction which is in opposition to your Inner Peace.

The good news is that the more time you spend in your Inner Peace, the more pronounced the difference feels between its emotional state and those states that are not in resonance with it. Thoughts that are in dissonance with your Inner Peace eventually feel more intensely out of alignment than they previously did.

The Self-Fulfilling Prophecy of Expectation

In a similar vein, you also want to apply the same discernment to the thoughts you hold prior to interacting with a particular person. That is simply because you do not only direct energy to your relationship with the person while interacting with them, but also at other times when you're merely *thinking* about the person and the relationship.

When you are thinking about the upcoming interaction with your mother, and you are already thinking about how she probably will act, and how her behaviour will probably be out of alignment, you are already channelling energy into the creation of that unwanted behaviour. Before she even opens the door when you go to visit her, you will have already started influencing the outcome of the interaction! You have already set the *expectation* of how your visit will go, and if that is the dominant focus, the state that has been energised the most, then the outcome of your visit will follow the application of the energy. Now there's a self-fulfilling prophecy for you!

You can't spend all afternoon calling up thunderclouds and then be surprised when it rains.

The Inside Job

The biggest benefit of learning not to attach to the behaviour of others, is the improvement in your emotional state. In other words, your emotional state is your confirmation of entering your Inner Peace. When you are in your Inner Peace, your focus *has* to be in resonance with Self, which means that thoughts of worry, resentfulness, anger and grudges you hold against people will melt away. They are just not compatible with that state, and therefore the emotions that accompany those kinds of thoughts are not activated. Darkness cannot coexist in the same place as light, it has to make way for it.

What people most want is just to be in a better emotional state, and therefore be in closer proximity to their Inner Peace. This requires no change in the people, relationships and your surroundings—it's all an inside job!

YOUR PRACTICE
Insights for Application

This chapter describes how to remain stable, as the Integrated Self, while interacting with others.

The Mirror

Your life experience, including the people who enter your experience and how they interact with you, acts as a mirror to your emotional state. If you are stable in your Inner Peace, you will not give your focus or energy to external events or negative behaviour.

Reaction Reveals Resistance

A strong emotional reaction to someone's behaviour reveals the extent to which that person is relevant to your experience and acts as a mirror to a pocket of resistance within you. These reactions are valuable information, pointing you to what is active inside you.

Stand on the Rock

If someone insults you, it is irrelevant to your emotional state when you are solid in your knowing of your true nature. External behaviour need not influence your proximity to your Inner Peace.

Influence Through Alignment

The person most firmly planted in their emotional state dominates the interaction. Remaining steadfast in your own alignment provides an opportunity to draw the other person towards their Inner Peace.

Do Not Dim Your Light

Never sacrifice your own alignment or move towards someone else's lower emotional state in a misguided attempt to "meet them half-way." A light cannot overcome darkness by dimming itself.

Cultivate Sensitivity

Over time, frequent thought patterns can become so familiar that they are difficult to feel or identify. Cultivating a sensitivity to changes in your emotional state allows you to notice when you are heading in a direction that is in opposition to your Inner Peace.

Watch Your Expectations

The thoughts you hold prior to an interaction direct its outcome. Expecting someone to be out of alignment before they even open the door is a self-fulfilling prophecy. You cannot spend all afternoon calling up thunderclouds and then be surprised when it rains.

It Is All an Inside Job

Being in closer proximity to your Inner Peace requires no change in the people, relationships and surroundings in your life. It is entirely an inside job.

CHAPTER TWENTY-TWO

Relationships in Resonance

IN THIS SECTION, WE WILL be taking a look at what relationships in alignment look like. We will not necessarily be introducing new concepts, but we will be using the knowledge built up until now and applying it to our current relationships.

The Most Important Relationship: With Self

The first and most important relationship is the relationship with Self, as that is the only one that can make you feel truly whole, and that is because it is an internal relationship like no other. When you are looking for something external to complete you, you will always be chasing after happiness, very much like a dog chasing its own tail. Some seek lasting happiness in a relationship, while others look to material possessions, a job or social status. And although these give spikes in happiness, they cannot provide you with lasting joy, fulfilment and peace.

However, you can have these things (including relationships) and appreciate them, as long as you can distinguish between wanting to *enjoy* these things and wanting or needing your joy to come *from* them.

What Happens to Relationships When I Am Mostly Aligned?

A stable relationship with Self significantly impacts all your other relationships and life experiences. When your emotional climate shifts, your current relationships must evolve to match it, meaning you will interact with people differently than before. If any preexisting relationship cannot evolve to match your new emotional climate, it will become increasingly less relevant to your experience.

This leads to a new, deeper level of relationship with others, as it is not maintained solely at the avatar level but brings the Self into the relationship—if you approach it from the perspective of the Integrated Self. In other words, you dissolve any resistance perceived when looking at the person or relationship from the Integrated Self's perspective, allowing your interactions to start to change.

Now you are not looking at someone and thinking of how they have wronged you in the past or what they are doing (or not doing) that makes you feel a certain way, because you have taken back control of how you feel, which also means taking responsibility for your own emotional state. This simple but crucial step really opens you up to connecting with people in a whole new way. You no longer base how you feel on the behaviours of others, whether they are family members, your boss, your teacher and so on. You are building your emotional house on the rock instead of the sand.

Desire, Resistance and Co-Creation

Some of these relationships can contain a fair amount of resistance because they evolve over many years through hundreds or even thousands of interactions, some of which are out of alignment. In most cases, it is your pure desire to have loving and resistance-free relationships with the people in your life, even if you have strained relationships with them at the moment.

Once again we can refer to the Experience Formula:

$$Desire - Resistance = Outcome$$

If your desire is to have a loving relationship with a certain person, and it has not manifested like that, then you know that resistance has somewhere, somehow been introduced into the equation by either or both parties.

The Tripping Point: Believing it is Possible

If you have a pure desire that you wish to realise, you need to believe it is possible that what you wish can indeed manifest. In other words, by not believing that it is possible, you introduce resistance to what you seek to realise, which slows the creation down or even stops it in its tracks.

One of the tripping points can be wanting to understand the mechanics of *how* something can come to pass. You might often find yourself trying to work out the details from the perspective of the avatar, and that perspective will often tell you that something is not possible. Therefore, when you find yourself wanting to work out the details, and the effect is that it is introducing discouragement, disbelief, doubt and anxiety, then it is best to remove the focus from the subject at that point in order not to direct energy into the resistance of the desire.

Of course, the "counter-belief" may be energised enough that you want to soften the resistance on the subject, especially if it pops up frequently when you try to approach a certain topic. You can refresh your understanding of transformative thinking by referring back to the "Thought Management" chapter we covered earlier on.

Your Inner World Brings About External Change

From our previous discussion, you would recall how the world acts as a mirror to you, and that includes what you see and experience in terms of your relationships and interactions with others. If your emotional climate shifts, the external world will follow suit to reflect your changed inner world.

Even though *you* are the one whose inner world has changed, you can still bring about change in a relationship because *you* are different. You will approach the relationship and the other person differently. You will also radiate your new level of alignment, and therefore influence how that person interacts with you, all of which works to shift the relationship in the intended direction.

If you keep steady in your alignment, you are best placed to create the relationship that you want to have, either by the transformation of the relationships that you have or by the introduction of new relationships that match your emotional climate.

Creating from Wholeness, Not Lack

It is important to remember that you are not looking for any person-to-person relationship to replace or augment your Inner Peace, as that does not allow you to build the relationship from a place of being empowered. If you create from a place of lack or resistance, then you will not allow the desired relationship to enter your experience. Either *no* relationship will come from such an attempt, or you may realise an *unwanted* relationship.

If a relationship is not a match to your improved emotional state, that relationship will lose its relevance to your current experience. In order to have relationships that are in your highest and best interest, the best you can do is to remain steady in your Inner Peace where you are in resonance with those truly wanted and beneficial relationships.

Ultimately, you do not want to sacrifice your own alignment with your true nature because someone else did not line up with theirs—no relationship is worth sacrificing your relationship with Self. It's in your best interest to give your energy to those relationships that are in tune with the intention of having an experience filled with peace, joy and love.

CHAPTER TWENTY-THREE

The Approval Trap

Pleasing Others vs. Aligning with Self

MANY PEOPLE ADOPT THE LIMITING belief that they should live to please others, whether it is to act in a way of which others approve, to have the right possessions to be seen as successful in the eyes of your family or society, or to marry the right kind of person and have the right calibre of friends.

This often strains relationships, as people resent the person or thing that "forces" them to act a certain way.

For example, you may hold resentment towards your parents who you feel have chosen your career for you, the person you should marry or the way you should act. Or you may feel anger towards your partner who you feel expects you to behave in certain ways so they can be happy and show love and approval to you. Nurturing this resentment, of course, further energises those thoughts that keep you from being empowered. And as we know by now, decisions which are not made from a place of being empowered do not take you closer to the life you truly want for yourself.

Family and society often instil these beliefs about happiness and success, leading us to base our decisions on gaining approval and avoiding the judgement or disapproval of others. However, such choices do not lead to lasting joy.

Material possessions, like a house or a car, might provide fleeting pleasure, but true and lasting joy comes solely from being in your Inner Peace. From that place you do not try to make yourself feel whole, loved and joyful by changing the reactions of others.

Whether you realise it or not, trying to change others' behaviour or reactions is an attempt to change an external condition to make yourself feel better. For example, you may look to get a new car that makes heads turn, or a job title that impresses others, or a summer body that makes your friends green with envy.

However, when we are talking about being able to truly direct your life and being in control of your experience, the only way to do that is by mastering the mind. This is where you want to spend your energy and time: the ability to direct the mind; not trying to control others' behaviour. When you are in a place where you are empowered, meaning that your thoughts and emotional state are in resonance with your Inner Peace, you are in a place where you can experience true and lasting joy—no manipulations required.

In a famous parable, Jesus spoke about a wise man building his house on the rock, while the foolish man built his house on the sand, with obvious and dire consequences for the latter. What this means for us is that it is much better to base our experience on something which is solid and remains consistent over time (this is your Self, the "rock"), than on the emotional states, thoughts and approvals of others, which are changeable, fickle and not under your control (the "sand"). This really goes for all transient things of this physical world.

Your relationship with Self *is* under your control. It may not always feel that way because of the nature of the thought patterns that are already energised in your mind, as well as the fact that most people are never really taught to focus with any precision, but it's true. Just because it's something that's not seen that often, does not make it impossible.

How Do I Prevent Myself From Trying to Please Others?

The easiest way to prevent yourself from going down an unwanted road is to look through the eyes of the Integrated Self in as many of the "now" moments as you can. In that place, you feel whole, loved and worthy, and the actions that you take will be in support of that state. That helps you avoid trying to compensate for the lack or vulnerability that the avatar feels in the first place, when it is disconnected from the Self.

Of course, no one is in perfect alignment all of the time, and as with all things resistance-related, having awareness (of your thoughts and emotional state) is key. You need to be able to identify when you go down a path of interacting with thoughts that lead to a place of vulnerability. Of course, the quicker you identify it, the easier it is to change the direction of your focus. You can redirect the thoughts around the topic or you can transform them, replacing them with directed thoughts and thought-commentary which are in resonance with your Inner Peace. With the right level of awareness and a willingness to act when something is revealed to you, you can catch yourself just as your mind starts moving in an unwanted direction, and quickly course-correct to get back onto your intended path.

What If I've Already Created a Situation to Please Others?

Sometimes, if we are not sufficiently aware in everyday moments, or did not know about being empowered and aware in the past, we may end up in unwanted situations because we tried to please others. For example, you may already be in a position where you are sacrificing yourself to gain your boss's approval, or you are already deep in debt because you've tried to impress others with your material things. What do you do then?

The first thing that's important to understand when you are in an unwanted situation is that *your power does not sit in the past*. No matter how much energy you try to pour into it, your creative power remains in the now. You are creating the present moment, not recreating past moments. You need to accept that. It is always true.

Acceptance is the Antidote to Regret

You *can* choose to be empowered in *this* moment, and therefore you can change your perspective and your experience *now*. In this moment, you have the ability to choose whether you are going to focus in a directed manner or on what was and therefore energise those thoughts and emotional states.

Practically, it means that you start by accepting where you are for now. *You are where you are,* and you cannot at the same time fight against where you are *and* be empowered to direct your thoughts and your life—empowerment is not compatible with regret, or blame, or anger. Thoughts of that nature simply syphon off your power in the present moment, leaving you weak.

That is why the acceptance of where you are is the kindest thing that you can do for yourself: it puts you on the road to changing your current circumstances in a way that is compatible with what you truly want for your life.

It sometimes feels counter-intuitive: accepting your situation seems to mean that you no longer want it to change; some might say it feels more like a trick, like fooling yourself to be happy. To many people, it makes more sense to actively fight against their current situation, but that kind of thinking comes from the avatar's perspective alone, which does not understand the value of alignment and how thoughts and empowerment come into play in the creation process. By not understanding that process, people often leave one situation for the next which is of the same essence, just with different places and faces.

Acceptance does not mean that you give up on wanting a different experience. Instead, it means giving up on the resistant thoughts about the current situation.

From the place of acceptance, you are more empowered to direct your thoughts and energy, allowing you to create the life experience you truly want. You allow yourself to hear your Inner Guidance. A path then unfolds where your perspective and experience shift, as opposed to running from the current circumstances. However, from a place of acceptance you do not *need* the situation to change in order for you to enter your Inner Peace. You now *allow* yourself to enter your Inner Peace, which brings about more changes that align with your improved inner state.

Giving From the Heart vs. Giving for Approval

There is a difference between not taking actions to please others and not caring about others, or not wanting what is best for others, or not helping others, which may be very evident to some and maybe not so much to others. I think it is worth calling out the differences, though, and perhaps it will further ignite an understanding of what this work is all about.

When you are looking to please others, you are doing so from a place of not feeling whole, or perhaps not feeling loved or valued, and therefore seeking validation. It's trying to compensate for the lack the avatar feels when not allowing and experiencing the connection with Self. In these instances, the "help" you are offering to others isn't really coming from the heart, and any "help" you provide may result in feelings of resentment towards the person you helped.

For example, if you are looking after someone's kids over the weekend because they asked you to, even though you had other plans or just wanted a quiet weekend, you may have been looking for the asker's approval when you agreed, and now you might feel anger or resentment when you find yourself spending the weekend doing something that you did not really want to do. You wanted the response from your friend, neighbour or family member to be one which does not make you feel bad, which just means that you were basing your proximity to your Inner Peace on how someone else behaved and their own level of alignment.

When you are already within your Inner Peace and you then think of others, you are in a place where any help that you provide to others will come from the heart. And because you are in alignment, the type of help that you can provide to others is greater than the help that the avatar alone can provide, because it goes beyond the avatar-to-avatar interaction and connection to the acknowledgement and assistance from one focused part of Consciousness to another. From that place you can even positively influence the level of alignment and emotional state of others. When you feel like giving while you are in that state, give freely—it will be tremendously beneficial to you.

It's not that you don't want to help your friend out, but if you are going to help out, do it from a place of being aligned, or align your mind and heart on the action taken.

For example, if you said yes to helping out, then direct your mind to see that assistance from your aligned perspective. The story that you tell yourself can either be one which results in resentment, or it can be one of care and compassion. In terms of your empowerment, the thing that will trip someone up the most is agreeing to action from a place of being outside of their Inner Peace and then energising thoughts that *prevent* them from returning to their natural state.

Not only do you open yourself up to further abundance through freely giving (i.e. with no concern, stress, anxiety or pressure, and no resentment attached to that giving) because you allow yourself to be a channel of energy to others, but you also allow yourself to shore up your own alignment by taking action when you are inspired to act. In that way you also become more attuned to knowing when you *do* feel inspired to act.

If you are of assistance to someone else and you do it from a place of not feeling like you *have* to do it, but because you *want* to do it, then you can feel how the action reinforces your integration with the Self. This is absolutely compatible with the state of your Inner Peace, and is the very best way to give to others (and yourself).

YOUR PRACTICE
Insights for Application

This chapter addresses the pattern of seeking approval from others and shows how to redirect that energy towards alignment with your Inner Peace.

Build on the Rock, Not the Sand

Basing your experience on others' approval, emotional states, or reactions is like building on sand, which is changeable, fickle and not under your control. Your relationship with Self is the rock: solid, consistent and always available to you.

Recognise the Approval Pattern

When you notice yourself acting to gain someone's approval or avoid their judgement, it is a signal that the avatar is trying to compensate for a sense of lack or vulnerability. The quicker you recognise this, the easier it is to course-correct.

Your Power is Not in the Past

If you have already created an unwanted situation through people-pleasing, your creative power still sits in the now. You are creating the present moment, not recreating past moments. No amount of energy directed at the past can change it.

Acceptance is the Antidote to Regret

Acceptance does not mean giving up on wanting a different experience. It means giving up on the resistant thoughts about the current situation. Empowerment is not compatible with regret, blame, or anger—these simply syphon off your power in the present moment.

Give From the Heart, Not for Approval

There is a difference between helping others from a place of alignment and helping others to gain their approval. If you have already said yes, directing your mind to see the assistance from your aligned perspective can shift the experience from one of resentment to one of care and compassion.

Inspired Action Reinforces Alignment

When you give freely from a place of alignment, without concern, pressure, or resentment, the action reinforces your integration with the Self. In that way, giving to others becomes a way of giving to yourself.

CHAPTER TWENTY-FOUR

Boundaries from Wholeness

IN THE PREVIOUS CHAPTER, WE discussed the need to please others and how it can lead to being taken advantage of. While the common solution often involves setting boundaries, this chapter explores a more profound approach: understanding how boundaries relate to inner alignment and self-empowerment, rather than just protection from external harm.

Discernment in Setting Boundaries

Typically, people set boundaries to protect themselves from being taken advantage of, often after several negative experiences. In that case, do thoughts about needing boundaries arise from empowerment or disempowerment? Do they reflect fear and vulnerability, or security and wholeness? Do they originate from a place of Inner Peace or its absence?

Initially, these questions might seem unimportant. One might argue that the ultimate goal (to feel safe and secure), is paramount, and the means of achieving it is irrelevant. But do both approaches truly take you to the same feeling-place? While the ultimate goal may be the same, the thoughts that you have *about* your situation impact how you feel *now*, and the situations and the people that you attract now and going forward. These thoughts really *are* two sides of the same coin, where the one reinforces being empowered, and is in resonance with your Inner Peace, while the other emphasises being disempowered.

The distinction between these is really important in living a life of self-mastery. You want to maintain sufficient awareness to be able to tell whether you are acting from within your state of empowerment or not. Sometimes it can be tricky, as you may think that you are focused on what you want, which in this case may be to feel appreciated, valued and respected. But you can also be so focused on how you are being taken advantage of and how insecure you feel, that you feel like you need to find a way to protect yourself. The emotional states and experiences of these are complete opposites because the perspectives from which you approach the subjects are complete opposites.

Ask yourself whether you are focusing on being whole and secure, or whether you are trying to get away (physically or mentally) from being treated in a way that you do not like.

To the outside world, the outcomes can look the same, which, in this instance, may be someone who seems to have good boundaries in place or is looking to put some in place. The difference is whether those boundaries arose and are upheld from a place of vulnerability or wholeness. While these may appear similar, the experiences are complete opposites.

Boundaries as a Reflection of Inner State

There is a fundamental difference between "boundaries" arising from a place of self-love, knowing your worth and feeling secure, and boundaries put in place to try to prevent someone from treating you in a way that you do not approve of.

Boundaries put in place from a place of fear on their own do not change how people feel about themselves, and therefore the underlying feelings of being a victim, feeling unworthy or wanting external validation which gave rise to the situation in the first instance still remain. And if the underlying feelings did not change, even putting up boundaries will not spontaneously clear up the internal turmoil. If the boundaries sufficiently changed how a person sees themselves or removed the focus from that insecurity sufficiently, then it *can* change their future experiences because their perspectives change, but often that is not the case. Boundaries can be a helpful tool if they assist in shifting focus or provide temporary relief during inner work, but if someone wants to shift how they feel in a *lasting* way, it needs to come from changing their inner world.

Having interactions that you wish to change is no different from identifying other experiences or things you want to change. In order to remove "being taken advantage of" from your experience, it is helpful if you can identify what thought pattern or limiting belief is active in you that gives rise to such perspectives in the first place. That requires you to be aware enough in the present moment to recognise when that emotion of vulnerability or insecurity crops up and to then identify which thought led to this emotional response.

You can also try looking at the situation retrospectively and seeing whether you can identify the originating thought or thought pattern. What makes the latter more tricky is that the thought and the resultant emotional response may become a little blurred if you are looking back at the situation. But if you do it a few times, you will probably start to notice a pattern of thoughts and circumstances that lead to those emotional states.

If you are able to identify the thought or thought pattern you sometimes trip over and can acknowledge it, you can more easily recognise it when it pops up and then remove focus from that thought, or you can soften the limiting belief every time it shows up until it no longer is an obstacle to you in that way.

In other words, by changing the thoughts you have about something, you can transform it in a way that you don't have to try to plug holes for all the different ways something unwanted in your inner world may be shown to you, as we've expanded on in the chapter on Thought Management.

The Ultimate Goal of Self-Mastery

To be clear, setting and maintaining boundaries is beneficial if you're frequently taken advantage of due to people-pleasing tendencies, and if it increases your sense of security. What I do want to emphasise, though, is that you shouldn't stop there if it doesn't change your relationship with your Inner Peace. That is where you'll find the worthiness, security and wholeness that you are looking for. As you view the world more and more from the perspective of the Integrated Self, you will also find that the need to please others starts to dissipate, which is often at the root of situations where you feel like you are being taken advantage of. This is just another example of the way in which your external world, or your experience of the external world, changes when you change your inner world.

Careers

CHAPTER TWENTY-FIVE

Cracking the Career Code

The Myth of the Predestined Career

PEOPLE OFTEN WONDER WHETHER THEY have a predestined career, like an explorer sent somewhere on a specific mission. "He was born to be a firefighter," we might say.

The job that you have or are aspiring to may indeed be tied to the intention of the Self, although not always in the way that people imagine. You don't focus into the avatar with the idea of one day becoming a lawyer, accountant, real estate agent, banker or doctor. You do focus here with intention, though, and your Self does have characteristics that shine through in your personality, and that often plays a role in the career that you choose.

For example, if you love interacting with people, you may enjoy being a receptionist or an events organiser; or you may enjoy helping others and become a doctor, or lawyer or social worker; or you may enjoy the creative aspects of life and become an artist, writer or actor. Therefore some of the characteristics at your core can play a role in the type of job that you are attracted to.

But even if you have not chosen a job which directly links to those characteristics, and you allow yourself to integrate with Self, those characteristics will come through in more and more of what you do.

For example, you may be an office manager, and you may enjoy helping the people at the office and showing them how things are done, both inside the office and outside of it, because helping others and imparting knowledge is at your core. It is what comes naturally to you, and is something that you love to do.

Apart from the characteristics of Self, there are also intentions with which you focus into the avatar. These could have had an impact on where you were born, to whom you were born, in what form you were born (sex, race, physical characteristics, disabilities, and so forth). Sometimes someone is focused here with an intention to play a certain role within a family or in society, such as to change perspectives, or to act as a healer, or to be an example for others, or to allow the creation of beautiful things into the experience of others through them. There are many different roles to be played in the world, and Consciousness has a mind to play them all.

The Core Purpose: Expansion and Fulfilment

The primary purpose of embodying this form is the Self's overall expansion as part of Consciousness. Simply by being here and experiencing life, you fulfil that purpose. You cannot "miss the mark" in that sense. This is often something people seem concerned about when they discover their Self: that they may have missed the boat and that it takes away from the value of the experience. But that is simply not possible, as all experience brings expansion.

However, you can allow yourself to *experience* more passion and more fulfilment in your daily life by allowing yourself to sync up with your true nature more. When you are integrated with the Self, you not only allow more of your core characteristics to flow through, but you are also more attuned to the things that feel joyous and fulfilling to you, and you allow more of these heart-fillers to flow into your experience. The reason *why* it feels so wonderful to allow these things into your life is because it is in resonance with your Whole Self.

Refining Intentions and Preferences

Based on your human experience, you can refine what the details look like of how you let these characteristics and broader intentions realise in your life.

For example, if you are passionate about helping people, and you allow yourself to sync up with your Whole Self, and you feel the inspiration and pull to bring more of that into your life, opportunities present themselves to follow that path. And it's not just about any intentions that you held before you came forth into this life. Since you expand through living life, you also continuously refine what you want your experience to look like.

For example, if someone's passion is helping people, the type of opportunities that become available to her and that grab her attention (and heart) will be those which align with her preferences and intentions *overall*. If she is passionate about helping others, but does not quite enjoy *physically* helping, but rather mentally or emotionally, then she would probably not consider becoming a nurse, but she may consider becoming a psychologist. In both choices, the characteristic of wanting to help others would be able to come through, but her preferences will lead her to prefer the latter. So she may have come with an intention of helping others, which is why she feels a strong resonance with that. But more than that, her experiences through the avatar may have led her to refine it to helping people emotionally.

The preferences, intentions and characteristics of both the avatar and the Self co-create your experience here. And when the two "minds" are in resonance, you are truly empowered and live life as the Integrated Self. To put it differently, when the avatar allows Consciousness to express through it, the mind and the heart align and create an experience here of lasting joy and true fulfilment.

The Power of Inner Guidance

The Self knows you—it *is* you—and therefore knows which path will be the best for you, looking at it from that broader perspective. If you allow yourself to be receptive to your Inner Guidance, which may look and feel like an impulse, a knowing, or inspiration, Self will guide you perfectly along your path. But you want to sync up with Self not only because it will lead you down a path that is in harmony with your true intentions, but also because when you do so, you already feel the fulfilment, peace, joy and love that you seek. It allows you to realise the emotion (feeling) that you are reaching for right now, without needing any of your surroundings to change. And in response to the shift in your inner state and what you broadcast to the world, your experience and your surroundings will shift as well. Such a change in your outer world *may* include the realisation of a job, new experiences, different interactions, and more.

It is helpful to keep in mind that a job is but one path, one channel that can be used to express the Self. The life path we are talking about here is one of the Integrated Self, which leads to *life itself* becoming integrated. Therefore, regardless of what you are doing in this moment, or what keeps you busy, you *can* live an Integrated *life*. Whether you are a full-time parent, in-between jobs, an executive, or a restaurant server, you can be an expression of Consciousness right where you are. It is all about whether you allow yourself to sync up with your Whole Self in most of your nows. If you are resisting where you are or what you do, you disallow integration with your Whole Self, and therefore prevent yourself from entering your Inner Peace.

Moving from Resistance to Attraction (Push vs. Pull)

Does that mean that you are supposed to stay where you are, because wanting to leave your job means that you are in resistance to it?

No. And here's why.

You are an ever-expanding and eternal Being, and therefore it is natural for you to seek out new experiences. As you live life, you also refine which things you enjoy, as well as the things you do not want to perpetuate in your experience. When you consider leaving a situation, you need to ask yourself whether you are leaving because you are resisting where you are or what you do (push factors) or whether you are feeling drawn to move in another direction (pull factors). Of course, there are situations out there that you absolutely need to leave for your own safety, but those are not the ones I am referring to here.

The main reason for asking yourself the question is because your outer world could be reflecting resistance within yourself. When that is the case and you move to another job without softening or releasing the resistance within, your world will continue to reflect the resistance to you. That means that if you were overworked in your first job because you were trying to please those around you, at the next job you will still feel that way, and the new situation and people there will again be catalysts for you to continue feeling that way. Too often, people are *running from themselves* in relationships, in jobs, and in life. That never works, and for obvious reasons. Truly changing a situation comes from first changing your inner world, so that your outer world reflection (experience) can change. Again, lasting change is an inside job!

Because you are always in the process of expanding, your preferences change over time and your emotional climate can also shift. It is only natural to think that, over time, you will start to be in harmony with different things, different people and different situations, as your external world begins to change to match the change from within. This can lead to you feeling a pull to move on to something different, or the situation might even change without action on your part.

In a career context, this can mean finding a new role, a new employer, moving to a different team, moving locations, or starting your own business. It can also be the case that your supervisor changes, the way people interact with you changes or you may be let go from your job even. Change can come in many forms, but making changes as the Integrated Self is the way to make those changes in harmony with what is in your highest and best interest.

In the following sections, we will spend the time to further unpack what you are enthusiastic about and how you can allow that to be a part of your experience.

CHAPTER TWENTY-SIX

Discovering Your Career Spark

How Do I Know What I'm Passionate About?

IN ORDER TO FIND OUT what you are passionate about, you merely need to ask the question, but the catch is that you need to be in a place where you can hear the answer. That means that you allow yourself to go on a journey of self-discovery, where you are able to identify and honestly acknowledge the preferences that you have. After all, no one knows better what's in your heart than you do!

So often, people are in a place where they will not even admit to themselves what they truly desire. They are trying to live a life that isn't a reflection of who they truly are. This is often a result of those limiting beliefs that we adopt from those around us while we are growing up—those Shackles of Society that we discussed earlier on.

This is why this question needs to be answered in a manner which does not activate the resistance of those beliefs as soon as you dare to ask it. This can be done by removing the part of the topic that acts as a trigger to activate those resistant thoughts.

For example, you could get a better understanding of what you really want to do in terms of a career by asking: *How would I be spending my days if money was no object and nobody else had any say or opinion on the matter?*

Initially, you may think that you would be spending your days lying on the couch, just doing nothing. Many people feel this way when they lack relaxation time. But once you're all rested up and start to feel like doing *something* with your days, how would you actually like to spend them? What would be *truly* fulfilling to you? What would you *want* to do if you did not feel like there was anything you absolutely *had* to do?

Some may even find it uncomfortable to let their thoughts be that free, and to allow themselves to think about what would be fulfilling to them. When we're children, these decisions about what to do with our lives are often based on others' expectations, and later on income considerations, generally speaking. It's not often that people base this kind of decision on some true and honest reflection about who they are and what they are truly enthusiastic about. Also, by the time such decisions are made (like choosing what to study in college), people are often still in search of their identities and don't know themselves well enough to make these kinds of decisions that will impact their futures.

Why We Overlook Our Heart's Desires

Most people live as the avatar alone, and therefore are concerned with the things of the avatar. It's understandable that people promote what they associate with, and deem important for, a "successful" life. And when your parents, family, friends, teacher or supervisor share with you their perspectives of what makes for a successful life, and it contradicts your own convictions, do not fight against it. If you do that, you will only sacrifice your own empowerment and move outside of your Inner Peace.

That is something that people often don't recognise: that which you *fight against* will always pull you towards a place of dissonance. In this case, it may be a state of concern about the future.

Instead, recognise that they're acting with the best intentions based on their knowledge. Quite often, those around you are well-meaning when they share their perspectives on success with you, as they want you to have a good life.

For example, most parents do not want their children to have difficult lives, especially financially, and therefore may voice their opinions on appropriate careers rather strongly. And yes, sometimes it won't come just from a pure motive to have what's best for their children, but might be coloured by secondary incentives, like gaining approval from their friends and colleagues.

Still, their motives should not be of concern to you—their belief system and their relationship with their Inner Peace are not your responsibilities. But that goes both ways, so keep in mind that you cannot hold them accountable for your level of alignment. Alignment is ultimately a one-person job. It is the relationship you have with Self, and by bringing any other variable—be it a person, event, or circumstance—into the equation, you assign the control over your alignment to others.

Yes, everyone has a history, and it's often easiest to blame others for the way they are feeling now, or the job they have, or the way they feel in their current job, or in their relationship. Ultimately, though, it is not the conditions or circumstances that are responsible for the unwanted emotional state, but rather the way you focus in response to the conditions or circumstances that is the root of the unwanted emotional state. As always, it comes down to your perspective!

It is this lack of understanding of where true happiness and emotional suffering come from that brings society to the beliefs that certain conditions lead to a happy life. That is how most people end up on the "hamster wheel" where they take endless actions, spending all their energy in pursuit of something that cannot be found outside of them.

In other words, the focus is on the things that society says will make you successful, and therefore happy, without sufficient consideration for the things that resonate with *your* heart. They have not yet come to the understanding that they can simply focus themselves back into their Inner Peace where true joy and inner wisdom exist, so that they can answer the question: *what do I really want to do with my life?* Importantly, from this aligned perspective, they will not look for that pure desire to bring them happiness and peace. They will know that harmony is solely uncovered from within, and that anything more that you get in this physical world is simply an add-on.

YOUR PRACTICE
Insights for Application

This chapter invites you to discover what truly fulfils you by removing the filters of expectation, financial pressure and social conditioning that obscure your heart's desires.

Ask the Right Question

To uncover what you are truly passionate about, it can help to remove the resistance that clouds the answer. Ask yourself: "How would I be spending my days if money was no object and nobody else had any say or opinion on the matter?" Allow yourself to answer honestly, without judgement.

Recognise the Shackles

Many career decisions are shaped by the expectations of family, society and limiting beliefs adopted in childhood. Recognising them is the first step to seeing past them.

Step Off the Hamster Wheel

The pursuit of conditions that society associates with happiness (status, salary, possessions) cannot lead to lasting joy. When you return to your Inner Peace, you access the inner wisdom needed to answer the question: what do I really want to do with my life?

Everything Else is an Add-On

From your aligned perspective, you will not look for a career to bring you happiness and peace. You will know that harmony is uncovered from within, and that anything more you experience in this physical world is simply an add-on.

CHAPTER TWENTY-SEVEN

Charting a New Course

How to Be Sure Your Desire for Change is Aligned

IF YOU ARE WONDERING IF you may be drawn to something, and whether that "pull" is in your highest and best interest, then you need to consider its origin. Does it come from the Integrated Self and Inner Guidance, or does it come from the avatar's fear, insecurity or vulnerability?

When you think about the opportunity to move on to something else, how does that thought feel in relation to your Inner Peace? In other words, what is the emotional state that accompanies that thought? Is it a thought that remains when you know that you are looking from the perspective of the Integrated Self?

Answering these questions reveals whether you're resisting your current situation (push factors) or moving purposefully as your Integrated Self, aligned with your pure desires (pull factors).

We are complex beings, so keep in mind that one topic may be influenced by both a push *and* a pull effect at the same time. That's okay. It does mean you may have to dig through a few layers to determine where the thoughts are predominantly coming from.

For example, if the thought of moving towards something else is joyfully exciting and pleasing, then you know that it is predominantly enthusiasm to take a step in the direction of a pure desire. If your first thought is that it feels like relief, then you may need to take a step further because it is not clear yet from where the thought arises. So you may ask yourself: "Why am I relieved?" And here, your answer can give you an idea of what is dominant.

Do you feel relieved because you won't have to do or see or deal with something or someone anymore? Or do you feel relief because you will have more time or a better opportunity to do something that you are passionate about? The first case here is driven by push factors, while the second case feels more like pull factors. These are only examples of how to approach the self-searching process, as each person's circumstances will be unique. Luckily, we all came with Inner Guidance so each of us can perform this level of inquiry for ourselves, tailored to who we are and where we are on our path.

When refining your awareness of your relationship with Inner Peace, note that simply asking a question can signal some resistance. In this case, the fact that there isn't clarity (by the person not being sure whether they are being drawn to something) means that there is some level of doubt on the subject. Maybe there's doubt as to whether they will be successful, or whether something will indeed be better. Maybe it's a deeper doubt coming from a limiting belief that they've held for a long time that they would want to clear up.

What our questioner will find is that when they are *purely* looking from the perspective of the Integrated Self, the doubt will either dissipate and they will have more certainty around moving forward, or the question will feel incompatible with the Inner Peace state, in which case they will know it arose from a thought pattern that is not part of their empowered state.

The Trap of Unempowered Action

The reason for analysing where a thought or question comes from is to determine whether you are making a decision from an empowered state. We know by now that decisions that are made while you are empowered help you follow a path of true fulfilment, while making decisions or taking actions while you are not empowered can perpetuate or even amplify the unwanted emotional state from which you are making the decision. This is but one way in which your external world reflects your inner world.

Still, taking action when you are not empowered does not mean impending doom and gloom, but as your inner world has not changed, whatever you are running away from or fighting against can be reflected to you again in some form in the new place or situation. You can run away from situations and people, but you cannot run away from yourself, your true self, or your beliefs. These you will always carry with you to the new situation, and unless you have changed your perspective and shifted your inner state, you will simply remake your new situation into something fundamentally indistinguishable from the old one. I've said it before, and I'll say it again: you are, at your core, a powerful creator, and you will keep recreating your outer reality to match your inner reality, no matter how many times you run away to something new.

Sometimes it does happen that an external change acts as a catalyst for a shift in perspective—a lucky nudge, as it were—where this change might end up being a lasting one. This is not the norm, however.

Most people have very practised and very energised thought patterns that govern their lives, and the odd lucky nudge is mostly not up to the task of changing your experience and empowering your now.

The only way to achieve lasting change and immediate relief, without waiting for external circumstances to improve, is to change your relationship with the situation *in this moment*. Once you change your relationship with the subject, change in your outer reality often comes in ways that you did not even consider, or thought was possible.

For example, from where you stand you may think that the only way out of an unsatisfying situation at work is for you to look for a new job. But once you see the situation differently, you may come to see that it was never the situation at work that made you unhappy, but only the particular way in which you *viewed* the situation that caused the turmoil within. If someone doesn't like you at work, ask yourself why you would choose to sacrifice your own alignment because of that. If you do that, it means that you have attached to the other person's behaviour, and the thoughts *about* their behaviour are not in resonance with the thoughts of Self. That is easier to see when you look at the situation from the perspective of the Integrated Self.

By living more of your moments as the Integrated Self, you may notice people interact differently with you because you *influence* those around you from this improved state. And even if *they* don't shift, your perception of them sure does!

Acceptance is the First Step to Freedom

In any situation, the crucial first step to change is accepting your current reality. You cannot be empowered *and* fight against where you are at the same time. The moment that you resist a situation, you sacrifice your alignment, and therefore move from the perspective of the Integrated Self to the perspective of the avatar alone.

You first have to make peace with where you are without judgement of the present moment. Then, if you truly release all resistance and accept *what is*, it doesn't matter whether the situation changes or not, because you are *at peace* regardless of your surroundings.

The irony is that people are often hesitant to accept *what is* because it feels like defeat to them. They are worried that if they become at peace while they are in a specific situation, the situation will not change because they accepted it, but the contrary is actually true. When you no longer fight against what is, you release resistance, and that allows true change to come into your experience. Remember how the Experience Formula works, and how you influence the outcome that you get. What you see in the world as a reflection changes in response to the releasing of the resistance.

There are also many people who do not make any changes even though they can *feel* that something is not quite "right". When this happens, people become more miserable about work; they may start feeling depressed, more and more health issues may start to pop up, they may wish for the time to be over, counting down the days or years to the next vacation or retirement. Under those conditions, they are not truly living. They are effectively keeping themselves from their own Inner Peace and not allowing Consciousness to flow through them. They have perhaps come to a false belief that life is supposed to be hard and without joy, and they hold themselves captive in that belief. Or they believe that their happiness depends on the circumstances and people around them. Whatever the specific belief, there are energised thought patterns of an unwanted emotional state which are dominant in those experiences, and unless there is a change in perspective, the current trend will continue and even be amplified over time.

The changes that we speak about here, of course, refer to changing the relationship with Self, in order for you to be empowered. By having a relationship with Self where you are receptive to allowing joy and peace into your experience, you also build an awareness to know where you are in relation to your Inner Peace in any moment, and to be in a place where you can receive the ideas, inspiration and thoughts flowing to you from your Creative Source.

Again, if someone is not in that place, it does not mean that the person's life is then a "failure". It cannot be, for they are here experiencing life, and therefore their Whole Self, and Consciousness, are still expanding.

However, the experience of the avatar could be less bumpy. From the perspective of the Self, there is no animosity, no regret, no penance needed. For the eternal expanse that is the Self, this life is but an experience—an expression of love. There is nothing but appreciation for this moment and for the experience.

What is a Pure Desire?

A pure desire is a desire that is resistance-free. That means that it is a desire that remains when it is looked at while you are in your Inner Peace, looking through the eyes of Self. Perhaps the most important thing when it comes to discussing a pure desire in the context of a job or a career, is to highlight that it is a desire that is free from insecurity, free from a feeling of lack, and free from anger and resentment and the illusion of captivity.

Pure desires are in resonance with your true nature.

Imagine that you have been working at a company for a certain number of years and you are contemplating what you want next for yourself; the time feels right to reconsider where you work and what you do. Suppose your main consideration for now is that you want to live with more abundance.

Of course, there's no natural resistance in the thought of living abundantly, but quite often people have limiting beliefs that are activated when they approach the concept of money or abundance.

So, you tell yourself you want to find a job or get a promotion which results in *more* money. Now, if you were to ask *why* you want more money, you would get a better idea of the root of the thought, and whether the thought originates from a place of need or expansion.

For example, if you say that you want more money in order to be able to be seen as successful, that comes from a place of feeling like you have to validate yourself, which means you are identifying more with the avatar and less with Self. The focus is then on: "I need to prove my worth to others through how much I earn."

Or if you are in a place of stress or anxiety about money, then the perspective from which you are looking for something else is one of *need*.

Neither of these is a *pure* desire, as there is resistance mixed into the active thoughts on the subject. You'll come across a similar false belief if you think that happiness is a side-effect of having money.

Does it make the thought "evil"? No. But it does siphon off some of your creative power, leaving you with a level of attachment to your surroundings, and less in control of your experience.

So let's consider what a pure desire around a job or career may look like. You may be looking for a job in a particular industry because the industry gets you excited when you think about it; you feel drawn to it, without feeling that you have to get away from where you are now. You will notice there is no resistance in this moment when you think about your next job; you are not indirectly activating the thought pattern that you *need* the new job in order to escape the stress, anxiety, anger, and so forth of your being in your current job.

That is the value of acceptance; it helps to purify your understanding of your desire.

A pure desire can also relate to the subject of money or abundance. For example, if you do not have an underlying thought pattern of lack or a limiting belief when you think about money, and you look forward to your next position which will continue to *add to* your abundance, then you hold yourself in a place of being receptive to that abundance.

Remember that abundance can take many forms, such as job satisfaction, having friendly colleagues, material things and so on. All of these can be more readily experienced when you are in your Inner Peace.

The Power of Pure Belief

When you hold a pure desire from a place of Inner Peace, your creative power flows naturally. This is not abstract—creation is happening all around you, all the time. The question is never whether you will create, but from which place you are creating. This reminds me of a piece of wisdom shared by Krishna in the Bhagavad Gita: "The intention behind action is what matters. Those who are motivated only by desire for the fruits of action are miserable, for they are constantly anxious about the results of what they do."

Remember that what you are ultimately reaching for is your Inner Peace. When resistance falls away, the first thing you experience is a shift in your inner state, and from that place of alignment, your outer world begins to respond. A desire that holds little or no resistance can flow more freely into your experience, not because you willed it into being, but because you are no longer blocking what is natural to you.

It's really a different expression of cause and effect at play. Our thoughts and beliefs are not unrelated to our actions and how our surroundings respond to our inner worlds. For example, if you are a painter but have some resistance in the form of self-doubt, you may find that your creation process takes longer, because you may be in the flow less frequently. Two forces are opposing each other and have flow-on effect. In general, the more resistance is present, the more difficult it is for something of a resistance-free nature to flow into your experience. And should the resistance become dominant, what manifests can actually be in opposition to your pure intention. Just think again about how the Experience Formula works.

Of course, what you desire is also subject to your beliefs about the ways in which it can enter your experience. If you believe that something can only enter your experience in certain ways, then you effectively limit it to those avenues in which you believe. For example, if you believe that the only way that you can have more abundance is to work more and get a promotion, and that it requires sacrifice in terms of family life, then that is the way in which it will flow to you if the limiting belief is strong enough. In this case, you are not a match to opportunities outside that rigid belief—like a job where the work/life balance is significantly better, allowing you to simultaneously earn a bigger salary and spend more time with your family.

Many causes come together in this co-creation environment, and the form that creation takes is not always easy to predict or understand. What unfolds into your experience may look very different from what you imagined, and often far better. Fortunately, we don't have to figure out every piece of the puzzle. Your Inner Guidance sees a far broader picture than the avatar's perspective allows, and your part is to hold steady in your alignment, to soften the resistance, and to trust the process. The rest unfolds from there.

Practical Acceptance: How to Shift Your Perspective

If your current situation is very difficult, you may be wondering how to achieve acceptance.

It all starts by changing how and what you think *about* a situation. As you change your perspective, your inner state will begin to return to your true nature, which is free from emotional suffering. By de-energising the resistant thoughts about the topic you can look at the situation more and more from the perspective of the Integrated Self (i.e. from your place of Inner Peace). It's as simple as engaging more with empowering thoughts about the subject and focusing less on those thoughts that contain disempowering judgement on the topic.

Practically speaking, it means that you deliberately think different thoughts about the situation—you begin to tell a different story to yourself and others about it. So you may remind yourself of those aspects of the situation that you do like and emphasise the ways in which it serves you.

For example, even if you do not wish to remain in your current job for very long, you can recognise that in this moment it is a source of income for you, and therefore it does serve you in the now. Perhaps you also gained experience or skills which will serve you in your next job. Perhaps you made a friend or built a supportive network where you are. Maybe you were shown where you still carry resistance with you, which offers you an opportunity to release thought patterns which do not serve you. And from this experience you may now know more clearly what you *truly* value. If your current job requires a lot of overtime, you may now know more clearly that you value time off to go hike in the mountains more than the prestige that comes from working at this specific company, or the job title, or the additional money, whatever the case may be. By being aware of how *what is* serves you, you release the resistance to the situation in the present moment, and you take back your power. Using the *empowered now* and the knowledge gained about yourself, you can step into the place where *you* direct your life.

You can also detach from the situation, which means that you engage less with the resistant thoughts on the topic. You create a space between you and the situation. This may look like reminding yourself of the temporary nature of all things, including this situation that you do not like. You may also remind yourself that the situation does not form a part of your identity. It isn't a part of you, and it does not define who and what you are.

You can apply all those techniques we spoke about in the Thought Management section to help you during a time of inner turmoil, including becoming *present* more, which also means that you simply engage less with those resistant thoughts!

By practising to look at your surroundings from your Integrated perspective more and more, your practised thought patterns on the subject can change, allowing you to reach a place of acceptance, even appreciation.

You might ask why the Integrated Self's perspective would give rise to appreciation for even those things that you might want to change. The reason is rather simple: to the Integrated Self, the experience is valuable because it causes expansion of your being. From this perspective you can see how an "unwanted" situation causes you to know yourself better, by better understanding your preferences, and quite often you come to seek the Light and commence or reignite a journey of Self-discovery and Self-love. In doing so you can perceive the Self; for the Light would not be as easily recognisable as the Light if it was not for the shadow, to create a contrast against which the Light can be perceived.

From the perspective of the Integrated Self, you can therefore see the value in the experience, and how it serves your expansion.

As part of accepting, and therefore not judging, *all* conditions of the present moment, you realign with your true nature. It is only through releasing the resistance to the present moment that you can be truly free, and allow the abundance of Life to flow *through* you.

Finding the Energy for Change

Many people are aware of the things that they are passionate about. Maybe for you that is writing a novel, or painting, or making music, or volunteering, or gardening. However, people also often express concern that after a full day's work, or looking after their kids, or their elderly parents, whatever the case may be that keeps them busy, they do not have the time or the energy to pursue these heart-filler activities.

This idea is rooted in the assumption that time equals energy. Even when your schedule is genuinely full, what you may not yet realise is the extent to which you can allow the Creative Source to flow through you. You look for the energy within yourself alone, forgetting that these activities also act as conductors of energy. They help you open the valve of your Creative Energy. Not necessarily giving you more hours in the day, but transforming the quality of the time you do have and how it adds to the richness of your experience.

But it starts with being willing to test this for yourself. The Creative Energy is always flowing. You simply control how much you let in.

Now, you may have experienced this when you do get into the zone and the energy flows. But in the beginning you may struggle at times. Without allowing the energy to start flowing, you may decide that you simply do not have it in you to pursue your heart-filler activity. In that case, it is worth setting an intention earlier in the day. Then, as the time approaches, remind yourself of why this activity matters to you and how it makes your heart sing. Before starting, you may also look to specifically place your intention on syncing up with your Inner Peace to open the valve of your Creative Energy.

For example, let's say that you love to write music, but you also have an office job. You really want to have the energy to let the Creative Source flow through you in creating music. But you have the preconceived idea that you lack the time and energy to follow this heart-filler activity. This belief might even fuel feelings of sadness or frustration.

Instead, you begin to anticipate the activity throughout the day. Upon returning home, you actively focus on writing music that evening. Before starting, you engage in activities like meditation, bathing, running, or playing with your dog. Whatever helps you transition from the day's demands to the present moment. This practice opens the valve, gradually shifting your emotional state into harmony with your creative flow. You are now deliberately preparing the atmosphere to enter your place of empowerment and creativity, instead of leaving it to chance or approaching it from a place of residual resistance.

When you allow that full connection with your Self, it will feel like time moves at a different pace because you will get so much more done than you ever thought was possible. You are no longer creating from your human mind and effort alone. You are collaborating with something far greater than yourself.

YOUR PRACTICE
Insights for Application

This chapter provides the tools for discerning whether a desire for change originates from the empowered Integrated Self or the avatar's limitations.

Discern Push vs. Pull

When considering a career change, it can help to determine the origin of the thought. If the thought feels like relief because you won't have to deal with something anymore (a push factor), you may be running from resistance. If the thought feels like joyfully exciting enthusiasm because you're moving towards something desired (a pull factor), it aligns with a pure desire.

The Trap of Unempowered Action

Taking action from a non-empowered state can perpetuate or even amplify the unwanted emotional state you are trying to leave behind. You can run away from situations and people, but you cannot run away from yourself. Lasting change is an inside job.

Acceptance is the First Step to Freedom

In any difficult situation, the crucial first step to change is accepting your current reality. You cannot be empowered and fight against what is at the same time. When you release resistance to the present moment, you return to your Inner Peace, and your experience begins to shift.

Focus on Pure Desire

A pure desire is one that is resistance-free. It is a desire that remains when looked at from your Inner Peace and is free from insecurity, lack, anger or resentment. Acceptance helps to purify your understanding of your desire.

Creation is Always Happening

The question isn't whether you will create, but from which place you are creating. Many causes come together in this co-creation environment, and the form that creation takes may look very different from what you imagined. Your part is to hold steady in your alignment, soften the resistance, and trust the process.

Open the Valve

Heart-filler activities are conductors of energy. The Creative Energy is always flowing; you simply control how much you let in. If you struggle to find the energy, it can help to set your intention earlier in the day, prepare the atmosphere, and allow the creative flow to begin.

CHAPTER TWENTY-EIGHT

Weaving a Career with Passion

WHEN YOU'VE IDENTIFIED THOSE SPECIFIC things you enjoy, you'll want to bring more of them into your life.

However, depending on how you view your situation, your energy will either amplify *what is* or what you see yourself *moving towards*.

Directing Your Focus: Escaping the Experience Loop

What is is really irrelevant, in the sense that past thought and focus have created what is now. But how you apply your energy (focus) *now* determines what the future moments hold—so please keep that in mind as part of creating future moments. It may be rather obvious, but sometimes we overlook, and find it difficult to assess, the value of being empowered in each moment. While a single moment might feel insignificant, it's akin to a solitary footstep. Yet, the accumulation of these individual steps carves a path, leading you either towards your desired destination or an unforeseen one.

Drawing from our discussion about how your focus shapes your experience, it becomes clear why perpetuating the current situation is so easy. You observe *what is*, and therefore the natural response is to focus on those conditions and to react to them, which results in the future moments perpetuating *what is*. The more you focus on *what is*, the more of *what is* makes up your experience, and in the next moment you focus once again on it, and around and around it goes. I sometimes refer to this as the "experience loop"—the continuous recreation of *what is* without moving forward.

In order to move forward, you have to focus differently, in a way that allows the energy to flow towards the experience that you enjoy engaging with.

For example, if you wish to create a situation where you have more free time, you cannot stand in resistance to your current situation and complain about the lack of time that you are perceiving. That merely amplifies the experience of *lack of time*.

Instead, it's more helpful to focus on things that amplify the concept of *free time*.

For example, you can think of the wonderful things that you are going to do with your free time. You can also appreciate the current free time that you do have, and acknowledge the freedom that you feel as part of it (instead of using your free time to think about or talk about the *lack* of freedom). That is really the feeling that you are trying to amplify. Any thoughts that *feel* of the same essence will be helpful in directing the energy towards the realisation of that experience.

Sometimes folks use much of their weekend already thinking about how they feel bound by their Monday-to-

Friday job, which does not help at all to channel the energy in the direction that they would actually want to apply it, were they looking to actually improve their situation.

It is really as simple as determining whether your current focus is aligned with the experience you want. Continue focusing on things that resonate with that, and withdraw your focus when thoughts feel in dissonance.

Building upon this understanding, let's explore three general ways you can bring more of what you want in a job into your experience. The purpose for highlighting these is to bring into your awareness that there are multiple ways you can obtain more of what resonates with your heart, especially since many people think that the only way to improve their lives is to make a complete career shift.

The Foundation: Inner Peace and Acceptance

Before diving into how you can bring more of what you want into your experience, remember that the first step to changing your experience is to reach a place of acceptance about your current situation. That is the only way you are able to direct your life in an empowered way.

Also, if you are looking for your joy to come from the change in your external circumstances, then it is a futile exercise. You must first go inward to find your place of ultimate joy: your Inner Peace. From that point, you can create from the inside out. This is not new wisdom. A perfect encapsulation of this truth came our way thousands of years ago when Jesus told his followers that they should "seek *first* the kingdom of God and His righteousness, and all these things [the things that you want and need] will be added unto you."

The Three Paths to Fulfilment

Building from that place of acceptance, you can strategically expand your experience. The three methods below are career-specific but the concepts can be applied anywhere in your life.

1. Augmentation

The first way is through bringing more of the elements of what you desire into your current experience. We'll refer to this as **augmentation**.

In this case, it can mean that you stay in your current job, but because of your focus on what it is that you desire, you actively have more of those intended elements in your experience. This can be due to the lens through which you see the world, meaning those things are now highlighted to you in your experience, where previously you may not have acknowledged them. Also, the more you put your energy into your directed creation, the more of those situations will be created.

For example, if your heart is filled by assisting others and you open yourself up to become more of who you truly are, more opportunities will present themselves. This will happen not only at work but also outside the work context, where you can be of assistance to others.

You may join a committee or club at work, and in that way augment your day job with more things that resonate with who you truly are. Of course, in this circumstance the assumption is that your emotional climate is a match to the emotional climate of your workplace.

Yes, just like another living being, a collective of people also has a range of emotional states within which it exists, and as such, you may be in resonance with one group of people and not in resonance with another. That's easy to think of practically: you can see yourself joining certain groups, societies, clubs, teams or organisations, while you are in complete disagreement with what other groups represent.

The same is true for a company, and if you are not compatible with the range within which it exists and you are stable in your emotional climate, the range of the company may either shift over time, or else it may gradually become less relevant to your experience.

In this latter case, augmentation alone is not the only possible effect of a changed emotional climate, but a bigger shift will be reflected in your experience where you and the employer will play lesser and lesser roles to each other, and the relationship will end one way or another. In other words, you simply are not compatible with each other anymore.

2. Supplementation

The second manner you can bring more of what you want into your experience in a career context is through **supplementation**. With supplementation, you look to remain in your current job or role. Maybe due to circumstances, you can't augment your situation sufficiently, so you decide to start a project on the side. In that way, you supplement your exposure to your passions, potentially using this as an additional means of earning an income.

For example, let's say you are really passionate about baking but currently work in an office. Through augmentation, you might organise bake days and position yourself as the office foodie, where people come to ask you about cakes for occasions like Nana's 80th birthday.

Now, you may feel that the augmentation has been wonderful, but you want to spend even more of your time baking! So you decide to bake in the evenings or over the weekend and sell the baked goodies at the office, or at church, or your local grocery store. You get to do more of what you love, and it allows money to flow into your experience in the process, if you choose to. Supplementation can either evolve naturally from augmentation, or it can be a directed creation in itself.

For example, you can either decide to start baking specifically in your spare time, or by being the known baker at work, people may request you bake things for them, and in that way, it becomes a supplementation.

3. Substitution

The third manner you can increase your exposure to the things that you desire is through **substitution**. In this case you are replacing all or a part of your current job or activities with a new one. How different the replacement is really depends on how much change you want and how much change you've allowed to come into your experience. It can range from something very similar to your current job but in a better matched environment, all the way to a complete change of career, starting something new from scratch, or even going back to school in preparation for an unfolding change.

Similar to how supplementation can come about, substitution can grow organically from supplementation into something that replaces your current job in part or in full, or you can have the desire to do something that you are passionate about full-time.

For example, you might be so in love with baking that you gravitate towards doing it full-time; in that case, substitution would be a natural progression of the creation of that reality.

It's important enough to remind you that substitution should not be a result of wanting to get away from where you are, because if it is, you are approaching it from a place where resistance is dominant. Acting and deciding from that place suggests you are not making an empowered move when you are making big changes, which very often leads to a place where the emotional state is perpetuated, just in a different place or in a different form.

For example, if your emotional state is predominantly one of worrying, and you decide to leave your job in an effort to reduce your worrying about everything at work, then you will certainly find other things to worry about. Suddenly you will worry about how long you can survive on your savings before you get a new job, and then you'll worry about whether you will even be *able* to get a new job. You may worry about what the family will say about your leaving your job, and what your friends will think. Because you did not clean up the internal world before making the move, the resistance will pop up even in this changed environment or circumstances. With this continued (and possibly amplified) state of worry and inner turmoil you simply won't be in a place where you have access to your Creative Source. It will prevent you from enjoying what you actually wanted to do.

The result in this case is quite the opposite of the experience of joy and enthusiasm that you had in mind to begin with. And if your experience does not reflect your pure intention then you will feel the tug of war within.

Not Attaching to Outcomes

What's important to remember here is that even if you have a desire to do more of something or to do something else, your relationship with your Inner Peace should not be dependent on meeting that desire. There are two reasons for this.

Firstly, if you are to direct your life in the direction of what and who it is that you want to become, you need to do so from your Inner Peace, because that is where you are empowered. But remember, you do not have access to your Inner Peace when you stand in resistance to *what is*. Therefore, you need to first build a stable relationship with your Inner Peace and from there direct your steps. That means to be in a place of acceptance in relation to your current situation even before you make the change, and it also means that you are not pursuing this desire as a way to escape from your situation in the present moment.

Secondly, you want the relationship with your Inner Peace to be stable regardless of the circumstances and conditions around you, because that means that you remain in control of your experience. The less you react to the conditions around you, any of which can take you out of your aligned state, the more you can control your emotional state in this moment, which not only feels better, but also means that you are better positioned to influence the future conditions that manifest around you. In terms of the

Experience Formula, you are reducing resistance and therefore you can better direct the outcome.

One last thing worth repeating here is that directed thinking is a *skill*, and it is an entirely new way of approaching life for many people. It is like exercising a focus muscle that you likely haven't used very much in this way before. Sometimes you may focus on something that is not in resonance with your Inner Peace, but the more you are *aware* of when that happens and make sure to bring your focus back into alignment, the more the aligned state begins to feel like your default state.

People sometimes beat themselves up for focusing in a way that they did not intend to focus, and then their emotional states and sometimes even their actions reflect that. Remember, alignment is a moment-to-moment relativity to your true nature. When you happen to focus in opposition to your Inner Peace, that does not mean you have failed at alignment, or at mastering the self, or that you are failing your mission here. And it *definitely* does not mean that someone is out to punish you.

You can, however, punish yourself with your thoughts and keep yourself from your alignment even longer, and if you remain out of alignment long enough, eventually the world will reflect that state to you. You also do not have to defend your level of alignment to anyone else. Even if someone knows that you are on a self-mastery journey and notes that you are out of alignment at times, it is only a matter of your relationship with Self. Should they ask about it, tell them it's an ongoing relationship with Self that you cherish. Explain that you are getting better at it every day as you refine your focus.

Yes, sometimes the understanding of how it all fits together can "click" overnight. You might come to understand the relationship between the avatar and the Self, which you can think of as an awakening of sorts. However, that knowing in itself does not translate into being aligned. Alignment itself is a product of your thoughts and focus. To think and focus in a way that supports your alignment is a different kind of skill to master, and as with all skills, some may master it almost immediately, while others may take a bit more time.

Irrespective of all that, you are here living life. Through your experiences, you are expanding, and therefore you are already contributing immeasurably to the expansion of the Whole Self.

There is no scorecard.

Measuring worth or value through action is a construct of the avatar, so don't take things too seriously; you are not here to prove anything or get anyone's approval. You are here for joyful expansion and living life as an eternal being even while a part of your consciousness is in this physical container. And part of being physical and having a physical mind means that there will always be an ongoing conversation with shadow, but by becoming a master at focusing, you can avoid attaching to those thoughts that you do not want to keep in your experience. They can pass like the wind through your hair.

Making Decisions: Trusting Inner Guidance

In your day-to-day experience it is valuable to know when to apply more energy and focus to something and when it is helpful not to do so. Earlier we discussed how there is only ever this moment, followed by the next, and then another. And the only place where you have any power is in *this* moment. That means that even if there is something that you wish to create in the future, it all happens in the many moments leading up to the realisation of that desire, like a sum of all the moments.

En route to that realisation there will be inspiration, actions, insights and conversations, all the ingredients that come together in this physical environment. Picking the right ingredient at the right time to add to the creation mix may seem overwhelming, especially if you try to sort it all out from the perspective of the avatar mind alone.

What you want to do, then, is approach the various moments from the perspective of the Integrated Self. That means that you are in a place where you are able to let the Creative Source flow through you, so you can receive the inspiration and good ideas needed to bring the desire to fruition. Everyone who has ever tried their hand at art or craft knows that it is a lot easier to be creative when you are at peace within than when you are anxious or worried or angry. That effect applies to any creative process.

Discerning Ideas

So, let's say that you have to choose between different options, and you don't know which option will result in the best outcome. For example, you may need to decide whether you take a job offer you received, or whether you stay with your current employer. What you want to determine is the origin of the thought or idea.

There are a few ways to do this:

- You can think back to the emotional state that you were in when the idea arose.

- You can ask yourself what led to your thinking of that thought, and often you will get a sense of the underlying thought pattern and its emotional state.

- When you are stable in your Inner Peace, you can again engage with the idea and feel whether it is in resonance with your Inner Peace.

If you have two options, you can do all of the "checks" for both ideas and feel how they compare.

Now, of course, not every choice will be distinctly in contrast with your Inner Peace, because your path is not pre-programmed, but you will have a sense of the direction that you want to go in. Some options are equal or similar in what they mean for your experience.

For options that are equally good or neutral, you will need to choose an option and then — and this part is crucial — you will need to accept that decision (and the changes it brings) as the new *what is*.

It is when you start to doubt yourself later on that you introduce resistance into your experience. This is not to say that you cannot make a different decision in the future, but that should be done from a place of accepting the *now* and the decisions that led to *what is*. Regret and doubt simply act to disempower you in the current moment.

There are also times when multiple ideas may seem equally "bad", in the sense that none of them may be in resonance with your Inner Peace.

Here it can be very helpful to discern between amplifying your focus, your energy, and removing it.

When you are acting as the Integrated Self, that's when you should focus energy, as the energy is then applied in a manner that is supportive of who you are and what you want to create. That means thinking about the subject more and really engaging with the thoughts about it.

When you are not close to your Inner Peace, then you would not want to energise your current resistant thoughts and emotional state any further, and you ideally wouldn't want to take any big action step from that place if you can help it.

Practically, it would mean finding ways to change your focus on a subject by either focusing on something else (distracting yourself from the subject) or by diffusing your focus while you seek further clarity.

As such, when you are presented with options where none seem to be in resonance with your Inner Peace, it may be best not to take any action for now. After deciding that none of the options are what you actually want, set forth the intention to follow your aligned path and place yourself in the position where you can receive the guidance coming forth from within. That is, enter your Inner Peace as frequently as you can, as that allows you to be able to receive the ideas, thoughts and inspiration coming from Self for which you've specifically asked. Then let any action flow from there.

Directing Thought

Think about driving a golf cart from point A (where you are) to point B (where you want to be) across a wide open field. When your cart is pointing in the direction of point B, that's when you step on the accelerator. When your cart is pointed in the direction of point C, where you do not want to go, that's when you take your foot off the accelerator or even apply the brakes so that you can steer the cart in the right direction.

I want you to see your thoughts as both pointing in a direction *and* applying energy in that direction. By removing your focus from a particular thought or thought pattern, you take your foot off the gas *in that direction*. By engaging with different thoughts, you change the direction your focus is pointing. By continuing to engage with those thoughts (especially while you're in alignment with your Inner Peace or Self), you "hit the gas" and speed up in that direction. In other words, you energise that state.

So when we are talking about being in the right place to allow something that you truly desire to flow into your experience, we are talking about it in terms of your emotional weather and your emotional climate. As we said earlier, all that you ever have is the present moment, and you can allow yourself to be in resonance with your Inner Peace in the moment or not, which translates to being empowered in the moment or not. When you are empowered, you are allowing yourself to realise the enjoyable experience that you want.

A final thought on our discussion of action and creation. Do not *wait* for a condition to change in order to live life as the Integrated Self. Not only are you empowered in every moment that you approach life as the Integrated Self, but you also have the benefit of already being at peace with yourself and your world from the moment that you allow yourself to enter your Inner Peace. What's more, you want to train yourself to remain in that state of Inner Peace, independent of the conditions around you. That is how *you* can be in control of your life: by being in control of your focus and therefore in control of your current and future experiences.

A Final Reminder: You Have Only One Job

Even though there may be wonderful things that you have created, or are in the process of creating, I want to remind you that you only have one "job" as a part of Consciousness, and that is to experience life—to simply *be*.

You *cannot* "miss the mark".

You *cannot* "fail".

You *cannot* "mess it all up".

Yes, you have come with certain intentions, and that can result in your doing something like a specific job, and you will refine your preferences while you are here and can therefore be drawn to do certain things. That makes for a rich experience while living life as the Integrated Self, but you can live as the Integrated Self where you are *right now*.

You do not need a specific job, or to live in a specific place, or to be married, or to have the perfect studio setup, to live as the Integrated Self. This is an internal relationship with Self that makes the focused experience here one of joy, fulfilment and love.

But even if you do not let your life here be one that is lived from the perspective of the Integrated Self, still you will not have "failed" at life. The avatar could have had a smoother experience, and you may have grown in different ways. However, the core of you, the Self, is never in peril. It does not need saving, nor does it have a moment's regret about the avatar's experiences, because it is all still part of its expansion through this physical expression of eternal love.

By living *through* the avatar, and not so much *as* the avatar, it does not *have* to be an experience of anger, pain, worry, anxiety and sadness. You *can* live life from a place of peace, joy and love.

And that is ultimately how you want to live, because in your essence you come from love, wholeness and feeling worthy—all the core hallmarks of Consciousness, of which you are an integral part.

YOUR PRACTICE
Insights for Application

This chapter highlights that lasting change is an inside job, driven by the careful application of your focus and the shift from reaction to empowered action.

Escape the Experience Loop

When you focus on *what is*, you recreate *what is*. To move forward, you can begin to redirect your focus towards the experience you want. Appreciation is a powerful tool in moving forward with purpose.

The Foundation: Inner Peace First

Before directing any change, reach a place of acceptance about your current situation. If you are looking for joy to come from changed circumstances, it is a futile exercise. Go inward first, and create from the inside out.

Three Paths to More of What You Love

You do not have to make a complete career shift to bring more fulfilment into your experience. Augmentation brings more of what you truly desire into your current role. Supplementation adds a passion project alongside your existing work. Substitution replaces part or all of your current role with something new. Each can evolve naturally from the one before.

Do Not Attach to Outcomes

Your relationship with your Inner Peace should not depend on meeting a desire. Direct your life from alignment, but do not make your peace contingent on the result. The less you react to conditions around you, the more you remain in control of your experience.

Direct Your Thoughts Like a Golf Cart

Your thoughts both point in a direction and apply energy in that direction. When your focus is aligned with your Inner Peace, step on the accelerator. When it is not, take your foot off the gas and steer back. You energise what you engage with, and withdraw energy from what you don't.

Discern Before You Decide

When choosing between options, check the origin of each idea. Was it born from alignment or from resistance? If no option feels right, it may be best not to act yet. From there, you can set the intention, enter your Inner Peace, and allow guidance to come.

There is No Scorecard

You have only one job as part of Consciousness: to experience life. You cannot miss the mark. Alignment is a skill you refine over time, not a test you pass or fail. When you focus in a way you didn't intend, simply bring your focus back. No punishment, no failure—just an ongoing relationship with Self.

PART SEVEN

Well-being

CHAPTER TWENTY-NINE

The Body as a Mirror

IN ANY DISCUSSION ABOUT PHYSICAL well-being, it is important to understand that there are many ways your external world (of which your body is a part) can indicate what is happening in your inner world. Most people view the body and its conditions in isolation. Although you can describe and identify the physical cause and manifestation of a bodily condition, it is only rarely that the inner world's interplay with the condition is explored. That is simply because it would be difficult to measure such a correlation empirically, and therefore, healthcare in general (especially Western medicine) focuses on what is. We often focus on the symptoms of a disease, while the disease itself can be the symptom of something deeper.

That being said, there are at least some broader considerations given these days when you see how the scientific medical field is including the impact of stress and anxiety more and more as well as their effects on the body and recovery from certain conditions. However, the focus of our discussion will be more around the mind-body-emotion connection and our relationship with *what is*.

It gets complicated very quickly when you try to go into specifics, simply because people are so diverse, not only in terms of their physical bodies but also in their intentions, their proximity to their Inner Peace and so forth, that looking in from the outside with a general measuring stick is a near-impossible task. However, we can consider some *principles* and see how they may apply in broad terms.

The Physical Reflection

As discussed earlier, your body can act as a mirror to your thoughts and your emotional states in various ways. When you do not maintain awareness throughout most of your moments, then not only does it become harder to see how things come about in your experience, but you also don't notice when certain thoughts get energised enough to start impacting your physical experience. And similar to other ways in which life in general is a mirror, this can be such valuable information in terms of gaining insight into your inner world.

For example, if you are experiencing a lot of stress as a result of the kinds of thoughts that you've been engaging with about a particular situation, and you are not aware enough to pick up that the thoughts are causing you stress, then you may eventually experience a more noticeable condition that can put a spotlight on that emotional state for you. You may see it in tension headaches, migraines, or getting sick more easily due to the interplay between your immune system and your emotional state.

By no means are we saying that there is always a clear and perfect correlation between the mental, emotional and physical bodies (elements) that make up this experience. What we are saying is that these *influence* each other and it can be helpful to understand that interplay, especially when it comes to how we respond and relate to a condition in the physical body.

This general truth holds true: when you solidify your alignment by stabilising your perspective, you transform your experience.

Just like with things that you may want to change in any area of your life, your attention and thoughts make all the difference. However, you must be kind to yourself on this journey as it can be rather difficult *not* to focus on something that is in your experience, especially as it pertains to your physical body.

Changing the Reflection: The Whipping Post vs. The Flow State

When it comes to well-being, whether it's implementing an exercise routine, changing a diet, or prioritising sleep, we are often taught that success requires perseverance, pushing through and lots of willpower. Does "No pain, no gain" sound familiar?

I am not saying you don't need to put in the effort to achieve your physical goals; of course, physicality requires certain actions, like strength training to build muscle. But when we question whether "No pain, no gain" applies to Aligned Action, it really becomes a question of what we mean by "pain."

There are certain physical discomforts that are inevitable, like soreness when you step up your exercise routine. But that's not the pain that our work together focuses on. While physical discomfort may be inevitable in certain shapes and forms, the added mental anguish people often experience is not necessary. So, the question we truly need to ask ourselves is: Are we looking to create, or are we looking to escape?

The clue lies in your inner monologue. Is it one of constant self-judgement and shame, or is it one of looking for how to best take care of this body over which you have stewardship? Once again, we can see the difference expressed in the Experience Formula:

$$Desire - Resistance = Outcome$$

Remember this vital distinction: the true focus should be the experiential outcome. Both efforts may result in a body that looks and is physically stronger, but the emotional journey—the experience—can look entirely different!

The Whipping Post

If you're taking action because you're looking to feel better about yourself through the validation of others, resistance is dominant, and the energy of self-judgement quickly overwhelms your pure desire. You may find yourself burning through your willpower and looking at giving up on the goal as you become exhausted. Furthermore, the core desire to feel fulfilled, worthy and accepted will not truly materialise through the approval of others; at most, it may mask the inner emotional gap for a moment. In this approach, the outcome you truly seek won't manifest because resistance is the dominant force. This is effort without lasting reward—the whipping post approach.

The Flow State

The path of the Integrated Self is different. It recognises that the avatar's strategy of self-flagellation is entirely counterproductive. You do not push your body into a better state; you invite it. You make a choice because you believe you are worthy of feeling good, not because you are trying to escape a feeling of shame. This shift minimises resistance.

When you choose to move your body because you care for it, or choose nutritious food because you truly appreciate your vessel, you enter a state of Aligned Action. This is the Flow State, where the discipline becomes effortless because the action itself is in resonance with your Inner Peace. You may still experience pain on the physical level, but there is no mental anguish that follows. You don't have to push through to become worthy, loved and accepted. You are that, and you extend that same courtesy to your body. The action becomes the reward, and that is the only way true, lasting well-being is created.

So when you're looking to take action, pause and ask yourself: Am I choosing this from the Flow State or the Whipping Post?

Responding to What is Unwanted

The best way that you can approach *any* unwanted physical condition, in yourself or in someone else, is to first reach a point of *acceptance*. To be clear, acceptance doesn't mean that you are inviting the condition to stay forevermore. Quite the contrary! Because by accepting what is in terms of bodily conditions, you start taking away their power over you. So if the condition keeps you from your Inner Peace, you can see it as pointing out that you have not quite shifted your perspective on the topic yet. As such, the condition has the potential to be a catalyst for you to surrender to *what is* so you can regain control of your experience. And with that release of resistance, you also open yourself up to be in resonance with the Source of your well-being.

Furthermore, if you can see a correlation between your thought patterns and what manifests in your body, like how I saw a correlation between my levels of stress and migraines at the start of my journey, it can be incredibly valuable information on where you need to refine your focus.

But even if you don't see the correlation, or even if there really isn't much of a distinguishable correlation, the overall lesson will serve you well in all circumstances: you ultimately have control over your proximity to your Inner Peace, and by being in acceptance of *what is*, and therefore not being in a state of resistance, you *truly* empower yourself. That means that you can already feel better (emotionally) right now, and you can allow changes that are in your best interest to realise in your experience, which can include all kinds of changes in your surroundings.

Practical Steps: Finding Inner Peace Amidst Pain

Of all the circumstances under which you can and would want to redirect your thoughts, doing so under physical discomfort or pain is probably the most challenging. It's harder not to go into states of worry, anger, or fear when you can feel something *in* your body. And because it is a condition *in* the body, it is also harder not to associate with the pain or the condition and let it form part of your identity.

As we've said earlier, the avatar (ego) builds its identity from the conditions and circumstances of this world that surround it. That means that someone looking through the eyes of the avatar alone may see themselves as a "person with X condition." This may be how they define themselves and convey who they are to others, sometimes even referring to themselves this way. Once it becomes part of someone's identity, it becomes harder *not* to let the mind-commentary about the condition impact your proximity to your Inner Peace. In other words, it becomes harder to detach from the condition. That does not serve someone who is trying to change their currently manifested conditions. But that is purely a secondary effect. As always, your first, and only, priority should be to enter your Inner Peace, and any change coming forth from that inner shift can be an "add-on" to your shifted mind. Also, you may note that the more that you resist and focus on pain, the worse it feels, while relief often follows a softened focus on physical pain.

How to Redirect Focus Amidst Discomfort

As always, the key to entering your Inner Peace lies in the ability to direct your mind so that you do not stand in opposition (resistance) to the perspective of your Whole Self (and therefore your true nature). You can revisit the section on redirecting thought in this regard for the more detailed discussion and apply those principles to the physical condition.

In short, it may help if you can slow down your thoughts when they leave you disempowered. This happens when you focus a lot on the pain or the condition, or when your commentary about the condition is taking you to a place of feeling like a victim or feeling fearful. One way in which you can slow down your thoughts is to focus on other things in your surroundings in this present moment. So instead of being fearful about the future, bring your attention to things in this moment that will not contradict your Whole Self's perspective, such as focusing on your breath, the trees outside, or your loving pet. Being in nature is a wonderful way to become present and feel the well-being that surrounds you. If it is at all possible, it can be very beneficial to become closer to nature.

And yes, being fearful about the future is a way in which your mind distances itself from your Whole Self's perspective, because your Whole Self is not worried about the future. Even though the end of the physical experience is definitely coming in the future for everyone, it is not a point of concern to the Whole Self, because it knows your eternal nature and its everlasting well-being. Also, the intention was always for the physical expression to be a temporary thing, so the end of the physical experience is aligned with your broader intentions. This physical container was never intended to become a permanent experience.

Death is not the end of your existence. It is a return home.

There are countless techniques and ways you can find to redirect your attention from the condition or thoughts about it. If you have practised disciplining the mind, redirecting your focus should be within your reach. You can also try to distract the mind, perhaps by reading a book, meditating more, or spending time with people you love. All of these can help refocus your mind on other things, or no thoughts at all. This will be beneficial to you because it will soften the resistance that creates the gap (a rift) between you and your Inner Peace.

You can also focus on appreciating those things in your body that *are* going well. You may not be able to do this when you are in the midst of strongly negative emotions, as appreciation is a long way off from a state such as fear. But once you have shifted your focus to a place where the resistance no longer feels dominant, you can switch gears to adjust your focus to appreciating those areas in your life where you *can* recognise well-being. And it doesn't have to relate to physical well-being, especially if that is a trigger point. If you can realise that so many things in your body are still going right, it can help you to think differently about your body and truly empower it to change—if it is in your best and highest interest for the condition to change.

If you cannot get to a place of appreciating at least part of your body because it causes you to activate thoughts of non-well-being about your body in general, then it may be worth staying clear of thinking about your body for now. Instead, you may wish to focus on things such as your financial well-being, or the well-being you experience through the loving relationships with family, friends, pets and so on. You can even focus on the abundance of well-being in nature all around you! If you struggle to see *any* well-being around you, it may help to first just focus on bringing your attention to the *here and now* without judging *what is*.

A point worth mentioning here, which may be quite obvious from our discussions about directing thoughts, is that you do not have to follow every thought that crosses your mind. There may be many thoughts that the mind presents to you, largely based on its previously laid out thought patterns. However, if you maintain awareness, it is easier not to latch onto those thoughts. You can recognise the thought as something that has come up from the avatar mind, but it is not something that defines you, nor is it really part of you.

Also, just because an unwanted thought has come up does not mean that you have to relinquish your alignment. The mind may come up with thoughts that you do not wish to engage with, and that's where you get to choose your direction in that moment. Either you can see the thought as something from the human mind that you wish to keep (and therefore focus on it), or you can let it pass by using both your discernment and awareness. If you can see the thought as something separate to you, then you leave room *not* to identify with it.

A Final Word on Mastery

Mastering the self does not mean there will never arise a thought that is unwanted and incompatible with your Inner Peace. Rather, it means you are not led by your temporary mind. You are able to steer your focus to maintain your emotional balance.

Of course, a disempowering thought is not in tune with your Inner Peace, but the effect to remove you from your Inner Peace only "hits" when you become enmeshed with the thought. So if you maintain a keen awareness, you can notice a thought go by, like a cloud, without following it. I sometimes laugh at the thoughts that my avatar mind comes up with, and then let them pass on by if they do not serve me. In doing so, I am then able to maintain my resonance with my Inner Peace.

However, your emotional state and the typical thoughts that pop up are not completely unrelated. For example, if you are in a place of feeling good, you are more likely to have good-feeling thoughts come to you. If you are sad, you are more likely to have other sad thoughts crossing your mind. But due to prior programming where you've adopted certain thought patterns, you may have thoughts popping up based on what you are observing that can be quite varied from your current emotional state. You may be feeling quite content or happy until you notice the bill that came in the mail. This may activate thought patterns of lack, bringing feelings of insecurity or vulnerability to the forefront. When it comes to your body, you may feel like you wake up from a good night's rest feeling quite peaceful, but only until you remember that this or that may be wrong with your body. But once the thought has shown up, it's up to you to determine what happens next. You can choose to redirect your focus in order *not* to energise those thoughts of worry, fear or anger, and *not* to energise association with the bodily condition. It can also include changing your perspective, therefore reminding yourself that the body and everything about it are of a temporary nature. This is in stark contrast to your eternal nature. That perspective shift can assist in avoiding binding your identity to a condition or becoming entangled with thought commentary about it.

It is from this understanding that the Buddha said, "It is wrong to think that misfortunes come from the east or from the west; they originate within one's own mind. Therefore, it is foolish to guard against misfortunes from the external world and leave the inner mind uncontrolled."

Ultimately, a condition may cause pain or physical suffering in the body, and it may be a *catalyst* for emotional suffering. By the standards of society, it's probably one of the most common and justified catalysts in someone's experience. However, it's important to remember that the emotional suffering that follows is still a function of the mind, and something that can be changed, i.e. it is ultimately within your control because your focus is under your control. But it requires practice and discipline to be able to exercise that control—just like strengthening a muscle to move heavy objects. And in mastering the mind there lies boundless hope, because it unlocks ultimate freedom. You come to understand that *regardless* of your physical surroundings, you can return to your Inner Peace.

YOUR PRACTICE
Insights for Application

This chapter redefines physical well-being, moving it from a struggle of willpower to an act of empowered Self-stewardship, guided by emotional alignment.

See the Body as a Mirror

Recognise that your body and its conditions can act as a mirror to your thoughts and emotional states. Stress and anxiety, for example, can manifest as tension headaches or sickness, offering valuable feedback on where you need to refine your focus.

Choose the Flow State

You can choose to move your body and eat nutritiously because you believe you are worthy of feeling good, not because you are trying to escape shame or gain validation.

Shift from Effort to Ease

When action is taken as the Integrated Self, the discipline becomes effortless and the action itself is the reward. When action is taken from the Whipping Post (self-judgement), resistance is dominant, which is draining.

Practise Acceptance Amidst Discomfort

The most effective way to approach an unwanted physical condition is with acceptance. This allows you to release the resistance that keeps you in emotional pain.

Redirect Focus from Pain

Under physical discomfort, it can help to slow down your thoughts and bring your focus to things in the present moment that align with wellness, like your breath, the trees outside or your loving pet, to soothe your mind and lessen the emotional suffering that compounds physical pain.

Appreciate the Well-Being

Once resistance has softened, you can shift your focus to appreciating the things in your body and life that are functioning well, even if they aren't directly related to the area of discomfort.

CHAPTER THIRTY

Unshackled from the Physical

AT FIRST GLANCE, THE TITLE of this chapter may seem a little contradictory, because we just discussed at length how your body reflects your inner world. Since a condition reflects such an intimate part of you, and because it manifests in the body (which the avatar mind identifies with first), it can feel like a fixed element of your experience. In that way, the mind can easily identify with the body and its conditions.

This is, of course, no different from saying that you are your thoughts—which we've already established isn't "you". Instead, what we were saying is that your body can reflect what is going on in your *mind*.

Although it may be helpful to bring your awareness to what is going on in your inner world, it is important not to overly associate with the condition. Just as the body is not the true you, but an expression (creation) of the eternal You, so a physical condition is nothing more than a temporary creation.

Social Entanglement and Emotional Suffering

The world loves adding labels to things, and when it does, it tends to equate people with the assigned labels. For example, a doctor may become "Bob the doctor" to those around him, and he himself may also primarily identify with his occupation.

In a similar way, people suffering from physical conditions will sometimes start to build their identities around their conditions. And with that identity comes an entanglement in vulnerability and victimhood. A clue may be if someone feels that anything that trivialises a condition is offensive, as if it is attacking a *part* of them. They may use it to get most of their attention and sympathy, make it a topic of conversation, or validate their emotional suffering. That is, they may linger in the unwanted emotional state because they feel that it is socially acceptable, justifiable or perhaps even expected. However, in the end, anyone's proximity to their Inner Peace is a personal matter. So it does not matter how many people tell you that it is acceptable and even expected to suffer emotionally because of your circumstances, it does not bring you any closer to your Inner Peace. It may be a bit soothing at first, but it won't lead to a *lasting* shift in your inner state. In fact, it may even keep someone from changing their perspective because they are exactly where everyone else expects them to be.

There are so many scenarios baked into society where people *expect* others to suffer emotionally, and when one of these occurs, some may think that there is no alternative but suffering. Even long before one of these things occurs, they may already be suffering because of it. They suffer in anticipation of the situation, telling others over dinner how horrible these things are that are happening, including conditions affecting other people. So these things get built up in society to an extent where it is hard for most people *not* to associate and engage with a condition or event that enters their awareness.

Why is Detachment so Crucial?

Viewing a condition as integral to your identity can impede your ability to detach from the accompanying emotional suffering. This is because such identification fosters a belief of attachment, making it harder to shift your focus. It makes it more difficult to integrate the perspectives of the avatar and the Self, because the Self sees the condition as something not a part of it (something that is merely a temporary manifestation), and therefore does not suffer emotionally because of it. If you want to shift your perspective, it is helpful if you can disassociate from the physical manifestation.

Not only does it make it easier to return to your Inner Peace, it also offers you the best opportunity to return to a state of physical well-being. But don't seek to change the conditions of your body in order to enter your Inner Peace! Seek your Inner Peace first and *allow* your experience to change so you can live the expression of what is in your highest and best interest. That *may* or *may not* involve the physical ailment leaving your body. True detachment means that you will be in acceptance of either outcome.

Association with the body extends to your perspective on the eventual death that awaits you and those around you. But when you are able to view your *true and eternal* life in tune with the perspective of the Whole Self, you break free from a very common source of suffering, which is that of grief and fear for yourself and those around you.

That is what lies at the heart of the Buddha saying that enlightenment frees one from Samsara—the cycle of life and death, and the suffering that follows attachment to transient things.

How to Disassociate from the Condition

If you don't want to identify with a bodily condition, it is important to remind yourself that any condition is always temporary. Remember that even your body is a temporary creation. If you do not see life as solely existing in the body, then you also don't attach as much to matters of the body. Attachment, and therefore suffering, comes from the false belief that anything can be owned in this physical form.

You want to maintain heightened *awareness* of your thoughts and emotional state to know when you are engaging with thoughts that are taking you away from your Inner Peace. The earlier you notice your thoughts taking you in an unwanted direction, the easier it is to turn them around, as they will be less energised. It's simply easier to shift your focus and your perspective in the earlier stages of a train of thought.

Consistency and the Journey of Mastery

Does it mean that the unwanted thought pattern will be gone immediately and then stay away forever?

No, that is typically not how self-mastery works on a practical level. When you try to de-energise a thought pattern that you have energised over many years, it normally takes time, awareness and consistency to shift your perspective in a lasting way. Sometimes you may be on track, and sometimes not. And when you are off your intended path, it's not about telling yourself that you are in the wrong place or that where you are is inappropriate. Where you are is not "wrong". It is simply about wanting to take control of your experience here, and that includes bringing awareness to your mind and your actions. This allows you to build the discipline of guiding your mind and progressing your journey of self-mastery.

With consistent practice and discipline, the frequency with which unwanted thoughts arise will diminish, and you will also enhance your ability to step back into your Inner Peace and into your power. If you maintain a continued awareness of when you start associating with an unwanted condition in your body, you are able to distance yourself from it quicker and therefore return to your Inner Peace sooner. It's not about never seeing an unwanted thought pop up, but rather having the awareness and discernment to choose the thoughts that you want to engage with, as those are the ones that will impact your proximity to your Inner Peace.

YOUR PRACTICE
Insights for Application

This chapter describes how your true identity transcends physical conditions, which allows you to look beyond temporary bodily states and step into freedom.

Avoid Identity Entanglement

The avatar builds its identity on temporary conditions and circumstances, including physical ailments. It can help to not build your sense of self or worth around a condition or a label like "person with X condition".

A Condition is a Temporary Creation

It helps to remind yourself that any physical condition, just like the body itself, is temporary. This perspective helps to avoid the suffering that comes from attachment to transient things.

Challenge Social Entanglement

Be aware of the societal pressure to suffer emotionally in certain circumstances (e.g., pain, grief). While empathy is natural, choosing to linger in an unwanted emotional state because it is "socially acceptable" or "expected" does not move you closer to your Inner Peace.

Detachment Means Acceptance of Either Outcome

Disassociating from a condition makes it easier to return to your Inner Peace. But don't seek to change the conditions of your body in order to enter your Inner Peace. Seek your Inner Peace first, and allow your experience to unfold. That may or may not involve the condition changing. True detachment means you are at peace with either outcome.

Catch Thoughts Early

The earlier you notice your thoughts taking you in an unwanted direction, the easier it is to shift your focus, as those thoughts will be less energised. Maintaining awareness of when you start associating with a condition allows you to return to your Inner Peace sooner.

Worry is a Function of the Mind

Worry, fear and stress about the physical future or the eventual end of the avatar are functions of the mind, not the Self. The Self knows your eternal nature and is not concerned with the temporary.

Where You Are is Not "Wrong"

Self-mastery takes time, awareness and consistency. Sometimes you may be on track, and sometimes not. That is simply part of the journey. With consistent practice, the frequency of unwanted thoughts diminishes, and your ability to step back into your Inner Peace grows.

CHAPTER THIRTY-ONE

Unravelling Stress, Worry and Obsessive Thinking

STRESS, WORRY AND OBSESSIVE THINKING are conditions that are very common in our modern-day society, and countless people are seeking ways to try to alleviate these emotional states that slowly chip away at joy, well-being and empowerment.

Why Peace Feels Out of Reach

From our discussions throughout this book, we know that most of the worry that people experience is not due to immediate threats and mostly result from the "what if" or "what if not" types of questions that play out in their minds. Those types of thoughts obscure your Inner Peace. They are simply not compatible with Self who does not ponder, worry and stress, because it knows your stability and worthiness; it is filled with joy and love as an unconditional part of Consciousness.

And to some it may sound flippant to say that what they are stressed or anxious about is unimportant to the Self. They assume that means that the Self does not care about their problems, but that could not be further from the truth.

The Self is simply so stable in understanding your wellness that it is not willing to think less of you, or be disempowered because the avatar is not allowing the full stream of Creative Energy to flow through it due to the way it is focusing.

In other words, these worrying thoughts typically arise from viewing life as the avatar alone.

It bears repeating: the avatar and its problems are temporary, while you are, in essence, an eternal being; that is your true identity. And that does not take away from your value in this form. The Self valued expressing through the form of the avatar enough to experience life in this form. Therefore the value of physical life here is immeasurable. But the intention is not to experience form by sacrificing the avatar or being caught in disempowering thoughts. Self holds the light of Inner Peace for you, but the avatar can choose to enter it or not; either way, the Self still experiences life in the form through the avatar.

The crux of the matter is that you do not have to leave the avatar before you can again experience well-being, peace, joy and love; you can live life as the Integrated Self where you align yourself to the view of the Self and therefore see the value and beauty in Consciousness expressing through this form.

Jesus said that the Kingdom of God lies within you. You already have it, it's up to you whether to enter it or not. In a similar way, the Buddha spoke of the mind's true nature when he said that the mind is luminous, but is defiled by adventitious defilements. In other words, your Inner Peace is always there; it is only the thoughts and beliefs of the avatar that obscure it.

Most people don't realise that it is only through integrating your perspective with the Self's that you can truly be joyful and at peace. The chase after material possessions, power, authority, respect, approval, awards, praise—all the things that the avatar pursues to feel secure, whole and worthy—often leads to stress and anxiety as they pour more and more energy into that endless pursuit. Remember, these are the insatiable desires that the Buddha speaks of as being at the root of suffering. The avatar's perceived separateness from the Self, and therefore the mind's separation from the heart's true nature, feels like a constant pain in the background. It is a pain that people try to soothe in many ways, but no compensating action or external factor can bring about the wholeness they seek.

Obsessive Thinking

Obsessive thinking can further energise those thoughts that lead to the emotional states of stress, anxiety and worry. Obsessive thinking in itself does not directly cause these states, as it is dependent on the nature of the thoughts that you are energising. But if you do not apply discernment in the thoughts you choose to engage with, a pattern of obsessive thinking can start to form. The positive side to the tendency to think obsessive thoughts is that it means that you can direct energy (or focus) in a very strong way, and if it is applied mindfully, it can really help you to be a strong creator of your life experience.

Another way to think of it is that when your focus is applied in a non-directed manner, it can lead to a downward spiral into those unwanted emotional states. But if you apply a lot of energy (focus) in a directed manner, it can instead be experienced as enthusiasm and passion as you home your focus in on those thoughts and things that are supportive of the life that you truly want to create, and are in resonance with your true nature.

Strongly focusing can be a blessing or a curse. The Buddha described this same mind-trajectory, saying that whatever you are pursuing with your thinking and pondering, that becomes the inclination of your awareness. The mind holds the key to your proximity to your Inner Peace, so you will want to steer it wisely.

Moving Beyond Stress and Worry

A common pitfall for someone who wants to master the self is being afraid to admit to themselves that they have thoughts that have gone off track or that they are experiencing an unwanted emotional state, often because they see it as some kind of failing. Or they are afraid that by acknowledging it, they will further energise that unwanted state. In such a case, even though they are worried or stressed, they refuse to acknowledge it to themselves in an attempt to suppress or ignore the thoughts and their resulting emotions.

But being on a journey of self-mastery means you will want to maintain awareness and sensitivity to your thoughts and emotions. You need to be in a place to acknowledge and recognise them, not ignore or suppress them.

For one, it is only through awareness that you can know to redirect thoughts and turn them around before they are very energised. Also, thought suppression is not really a viable strategy, as it will burn through your limited reserves of willpower to suppress streams of thought for even a little while. You cannot build a life of joy through the suppression of your thoughts; it's not a sustainable solution. And you cannot suppress your thoughts *and* maintain awareness.

What you rather want is to acknowledge a stream or pattern that isn't serving you and then redirect your focus and thoughts in a new direction. Ultimately, you do not want to become enmeshed with the thoughts that do not serve you. You want to build a perspective that is empowering and in harmony with your true nature.

Inner Peace and External Support: The Role of Medication

Medication and building a relationship with your Inner Peace are not mutually exclusive.

Very often medicines can be a useful tool to help you regain your balance, especially if something has already become manifest in the body. At this point it becomes much more difficult to look beyond the "condition" to the wellness that is freely available to you. In other words, it is difficult for most people to detach from a bodily condition, because it's so "real" and present. In these cases, medication can often *help* you to detach from it by allowing you to feel better and making it easier to shift your focus.

For example, it is a lot easier not to have your focus fixated on your migraine if you can alleviate that migraine in the meantime through medication. Being aware of an ailment is a crucial element of our survival, but left unchecked, this can lead to an added layer of emotional suffering if the mind reacts with judgement and resistance to its surroundings.

That is also why prevention is easier than cure. In our example of the headache, it is easier to shift your emotional state *before* the next one sets in than it is to take away a worry-induced headache that is already boldly entrenched in your experience.

If medication is something that benefits you, then by *not* resisting (that is, by accepting) the idea of the medication, you can enhance the benefits you receive from it. Through acceptance of where you are and what tools you may need, you allow yourself to further integrate with the Self. Through acceptance you allow the flow of wellness to you and allow yourself the clarity to better know what is best for you.

Also, it is important to bring your medical practitioner along on the journey and not to make decisions without the necessary consultation. Like we said, medicine is a wonderful tool that can be used to help you step back into your wholeness and well-being, or to help ease something that is active in your experience.

However, I would not *replace* my relationship with the Self with medication, or anything else for that matter. I would seek to enter my Inner Peace first and approach the subject of my physical wellness from there.

Acceptance Based on Honesty

It's pointless to try to trick yourself about where you are in this moment physically or where you are in terms of your emotional climate and your relationship with the Self.

By doing that, you will simply end up making decisions that are not reflective and supportive of your truth. I'll let you work out for yourself where that will lead.

Seek a relationship with your Inner Peace regardless of where you are now. Step into acceptance of *what is*, and let the stability of your alignment help you see the path of wellness that is available and of most benefit to you. But keep in mind that the path does not look the same for everyone. This is because everyone is in a different place physically and in terms of their emotional climate, and holds their own intentions from both the physical and spiritual perspectives. Regardless of how something's come into your experience, through the power of acceptance you can embody peace, joy and love right here, right now. And as an added benefit of this empowered state, you naturally become in tune with whatever is in your best interest.

YOUR PRACTICE
Insights for Application

This chapter empowers you to break free from cycles of stress and worry by treating your mind as a creative instrument that you can direct.

Worry Obscures Inner Peace

Stress, anxiety and worry arise from viewing life as the avatar alone, often stemming from "what if" scenarios that distract you from the present moment. Your Inner Peace is always available to you, but misdirected focus can cover it up.

The Power of Directed Focus

The energy you apply through focused thought can be a blessing or a curse. Applied without direction, it can lead to worry and a downward spiral. Applied mindfully, it is experienced as enthusiasm and passion.

Acknowledge, Don't Suppress

Seeing worry or stress as a failure and attempting to suppress it is a common pitfall. Self-mastery requires awareness and recognition of an unwanted thought pattern so you can redirect your focus before the thought becomes highly energised. You cannot build a life of joy through the suppression of your thoughts.

Medicine as a Tool

Medication and building a relationship with the Self are not mutually exclusive. Medicine can be a useful tool to help you regain your balance and make it easier to detach from a condition so you can shift your focus. However, it does not replace your Inner Peace and your self-mastery practice.

Acceptance Based on Honesty

It helps to be honest with yourself about your current emotional and physical state. Trying to trick yourself about where you are leads to decisions that don't reflect your truth. Step into acceptance of *what is*, and let the stability of your alignment help you see the path of wellness that is available to you.

Final Thoughts

A Final Letter

WE HAVE DISCUSSED MANY CONCEPTS together, and I hope that you have found within these pages waypoints that will prove valuable in your own journey. This journey of self-mastery will look different for each person, and in the end, based on your own belief systems, some concepts may resonate more with you than others. Some concepts may also resonate more at different times in your life, as we are all constantly evolving. Ultimately, the details of how you enter your Inner Peace aren't as important as knowing that it exists and taking the steps that work for you to enter it.

You do not have to try to define Consciousness or understand it in order to experience it, just like you don't have to understand the laws of physics to experience them. So regardless of your beliefs, your Inner Peace continues to exist and will continue to call you to it. That means you can always *feel* your proximity to it. You can *feel* how you are empowered when you are in it, and you can *see* how more moments spent in close proximity to it make for a life of more peace, joy and love.

As you go through this wonderful and valuable experience of life on Earth, there is no better guidance available to you than your Inner Guidance. By having awareness of your thoughts and your proximity to your Inner Peace, you are fully equipped to face the world—and you knew this before you came here. And because you can direct your mind, you are in control of your experience.

How empowering is that! That means that you can live a life of peace, joy and love—it's yours for the taking, or more precisely, it is yours to *allow*. It is your *natural* state; it is your *eternal* state. Don't wait to achieve anything external to you to finally allow yourself to live in joy and peace. Choose to live that life now, as that is where life happens: in every moment. Choose to live in joy instead of suffering, love instead of anger and hate, and with an abundance of life instead of just tolerating life. Choose to go *inward* to find heaven. Remember, lasting change is an inside job!

Ultimately, we're all on this journey of self-mastery together, and everyone will be at different stages of their path overall, and either on or off the path in any moment, depending on the choices they make. So remember to be kind to others and look at them through the eyes of your Integrated Self, seeing them as Consciousness sees them. Like you, they are focused Consciousness on a journey that has variable proximity to its Inner Peace, but is nonetheless still part of the greater Consciousness. And if they happen to be off track, don't join them there—don't dim your Light thinking it will help someone who's in the dark. Hold a place of compassion for them and shine your Light to help them step back onto their path. You can be a catalyst for positive change all around you!

Finally, remember to be kind to yourself and to apply the same compassion to your own life and your own journey. Yes, you can be a Light to others, but you're not here to gain anyone's approval. And because you are an eternal being, you will always be expanding, and you will always be shaping and refining your own expression of Love. In the end, because you will always be on a journey, life is about living joyfully in the moment, in the steps along the way, rather than thinking that your journey will lead you *to* joy, like a pot of gold to discover at the end of the rainbow. The treasure you seek lies within; you just have to choose to claim it.

Choose Peace. Choose Joy. Choose Love.

Thank you for sharing this continuing journey with me.

Love,

Jean-Pierre Claude

Acknowledgements

No book is written in isolation, and this one is no exception.

To my spouse: you have been my steady ground throughout this journey. You read every draft, questioned every idea that needed questioning, and held space for this book even when it asked more of our time and energy than either of us expected. This book would not exist in its current form without your patience, your honesty and your love. Thank you for being my partner in this and in everything.

To the teachers, writers and thinkers whose wisdom is woven through these pages: your insights have shaped my understanding of life, and I am grateful for the light you have shared with the world. I have tried to honour your teachings with care and respect.

To everyone who asked the same question I once asked, *Why, despite having everything, do I feel so empty?*, know that the question itself is the beginning of the answer. This book is for you.

And finally, to Life—the physical expression of peace, joy and love.

About the Author

Jean-Pierre Claude is an explorer of the inner landscape, dedicated to the living embodiment of peace, joy and love. Following a successful chapter in the corporate world of finance and economics, he turned his focus inward to address a growing sense that something fundamental was missing from the modern pursuit of success.

What began as a personal inquiry, sifting through timeless teachings, diverse traditions, and his own lived experience, has evolved into a clear realisation of the lasting peace that resides within every human being. A Life Empowered is the fruit of that journey. It offers a practical framework for self-mastery that bridges ancient wisdom with the grounded realities of everyday life.

Today, Jean-Pierre continues to explore and share insights on conscious living. He remains rooted in the conviction that our most valuable discovery is the profound inner stillness already present and waiting to be lived.

Bibliography

The teachings and quotations referenced in this book are drawn from the sources listed below. Biblical quotations are drawn from multiple translations, including the Berean Standard Bible (BSB), the New International Version (NIV) and the New King James Version (NKJV), selected for clarity and readability within the context of this work. In some cases, quotations from Buddhist and other sources have been paraphrased or adapted for clarity.

Buddhist Texts

The Dhammapada. Translated by Eknath Easwaran. Nilgiri Press, 2007. Verses referenced include those on the undirected mind, greed and lasting peace, the disciplined mind, happiness following a good mind and retaining thoughts of abuse.

The Teaching of Buddha. Bukkyo Dendo Kyokai (Society for the Promotion of Buddhism). Kosaido Printing Co., revised edition. Passages referenced include those on misfortunes originating in the mind, desires and suffering, the hidden treasure within, the land of peace, the pure mind of Enlightenment and guarding the five senses.

Pabhassara Sutta (Anguttara Nikaya 1.49–51). The luminous mind and adventitious defilements.

Dvedhavitakka Sutta (Majjhima Nikaya 19). The mind-trajectory teaching: whatever you pursue with your thinking and pondering becomes the inclination of your awareness. Paraphrased.

The description of Nirvana as "unborn, unrivalled, secure from attachment" draws on multiple Pali Canon sources, including the *Udana* 8.3.

Hindu Texts

The Bhagavad Gita. Translated by Eknath Easwaran. Nilgiri Press, 2007. Krishna's teaching on the intention behind action and non-attachment to the fruits of action. Paraphrased.

The Bible

Biblical quotations are drawn from the following translations:

The Holy Bible, Berean Standard Bible. Bible Hub, 2020. (BSB)

The Holy Bible, New International Version. Biblica, 2011. (NIV)

The Holy Bible, New King James Version. Thomas Nelson, 1982. (NKJV)

The Holy Bible, New American Standard Bible. The Lockman Foundation, 1995. (NASB)

Key passages referenced, with primary translation used:

Exodus 3:14 — "I am who I am" (NIV)

Matthew 6:19–20 — treasures on earth (NIV)

Matthew 6:25–34—do not worry; seek first the kingdom of God (NKJV)

Matthew 7:1–2—do not judge (BSB)

Matthew 7:24–27—the wise and foolish builders (BSB)

Matthew 12:34—the mouth speaks what the heart is full of (NIV)

Matthew 14:28–31—Peter walking on water (paraphrased)

Matthew 18:22—forgive seventy times seven (NKJV)

Matthew 21:21 / Mark 11:23—faith to move mountains (paraphrased)

Matthew 23:25–26—clean the inside of the cup (NIV)

Mark 10:15—receive the kingdom of God like a little child (NIV)

Mark 11:24—believe that you have received it (NIV)

Luke 17:21—the Kingdom of God is within you (NKJV)

John 7:37—if anyone is thirsty, let him come to me and drink (NASB)

Philippians 4:8–9—think on these things (BSB)

Continue the Journey

Thank you for walking this path with me.

If these words have stirred something within you,

I'd love to continue the conversation.

Scan the code above or visit *www.jeanpierreclaude.com* to:

- Explore deeper teachings and guided practices
- Work with me directly on your journey to alignment
- Join The Further Shore community on YouTube & Substack

A Life Unlearned

The Next Step on the Journey Inward

If A Life Empowered showed you that life doesn't just happen to you, A Life Unlearned invites you to discover that you were free all along. The second book moves from empowerment towards liberation—releasing the stories, beliefs and conditioning that no longer serve your journey home.

Your Reflections

Use these pages to capture the thoughts, insights and questions that arise as you walk this path. There is no right or wrong way to reflect—simply let your inner world speak.

www.ingramcontent.com/pod-product-compliance
Lightning Source LLC
Chambersburg PA
CBHW021223060726
47590CB00005B/1615